THE
PARALYZED
MOVEMENT

Finding Purpose, Peace, and Freedom from the Things Paralyzing You in Life

AMANDA ZWANZIGER

Unless otherwise noted, all Scripture references in this book are taken from the Holy Bible, New Living Translation, copyright © 1996, 2004, 2007, 2013 by Tyndale House Foundation. Used by permission of Tyndale House Publishers, Inc., Carol Stream, Illinois 60188. All right reserved.

Edited by Catt Editing.
Formatted by Rachael Cox.
Cover photo by Janel Anglick Photography.
Cover logo by Emma Kinney.

Get Your Free Inspiration Journal Download

Don't just read this book, **apply** it to **your life!**

Please visit: amandamotivates.com/download

This book is dedicated to:

Todd, who helped me see it. You are my inspiration.
My kids, who made it worth it. You are my purpose.
My family, who let me be it. You are my reason.
My friends, who prayed for it. You are my warriors.

Table of Contents

A Note from the Author

WELCOME, MY FRIEND.

Before diving in, I need to fill you in on a little secret. I'm not who you think I am. You know—one of those amazing Christian author ladies who has it all together. The perfect hair-styling, southern-talking, Bible-knowing, God-loving preacher ladies who so many of us have looked up to for so long. The ones who've filled our lives with hope, biblical wisdom, and God for years. You know who I'm talking about.

But that's not me. Not me at all.

Because I'm you. I'm just a girl trying to figure it all out.

- Working too much. But not enough.
- Chasing a dream. But not reaching it.
- Making progress. But falling behind.
- Trying to lean on God. But battling my mind.

Sigh.

Yep. I'm just a girl.

- Who may sometimes lose her mind.
- Who's following God.
- Who's paralyzed.

This book is the perfect example. I'll admit to you that I have been completely paralyzed in writing this—you should know that it took me five years to get it into your hands.

I had been stuck in a state of complete complacency, despite the fact that God plucked me out of a busy corporate job to develop this ministry and write this book. He had a plan for me. But for five years, I managed to chase squirrels instead.

- The laundry needed folding.
- Marshalls was having a sale.
- Facebook sent me a notification.
- The dog needed cuddling.
- The drying paint needed watching.

Sigh.

If you are reading this book, it's because the will of God won over the squirrels I was chasing, and I got this sucker written.

It's also because I decided to get super uncomfortable and drastically change the course of my life.

I chose to have total faith in this blind mission.

I chose to trust in the power of God to remove Satan's grip on me.

I chose to no longer let Satan keep me paralyzed.

You all have the opportunity to experience the same. It's why God brought you here: there is something paralyzing you in your life. And God doesn't want you to remain there.

Perhaps, at this point, you are instead wondering if you should continue reading the rest of this book. Maybe you, yourself, are being tempted to chase a squirrel. If that's the case, I ask you to ponder this:

If Satan wants so badly for you to not discover what's within this book that he is tempting you with squirrels, then isn't it likely that it's precisely what God wants you to hear?

I'll bet on it.

Let's start the journey of *The Paralyzed Movement.*

Amanda Zwanziger

Amanda Zwanziger. Speaker. Author. Coach.
The Paralyzed Movement ™

Introduction

If only you could see what he sees. If you could see the future he's prepared for you and the future he's preparing you for, you simply wouldn't even recognize it. You quite possibly wouldn't think to claim it as your own because it would look so different from the life you are living. So in contrast to the future you are planning. So much better than the dreams you've imagined.

It would blow your socks off just to see it.

This future he sees for you consists of a purpose that *only you* can fulfill for him. It's your unique story, full of trials, tribulations, and victories. It's your faithful journey, full of giant steps of blind faith. And it's your gift, the God-given ability that he gave you to make a massive imprint in this life. A purpose so great that I promise can save lives.

It would blow your socks off to just believe in it.

This future he sees, it's full of freedom. Chains broken. Wounds healed. Burdens carried. It's full of rest, stillness, and the peace your heart and mind have longed for.

It would blow your socks off to just receive it.

This future is yours.

God's truth cannot be questioned, disputed, or refuted. Your purpose is guaranteed. Your calling is critical. But it can't be fulfilled without you.

You have to be a willing player. You have to have faith. You have to take risks. The pursuit of purpose lies on your shoulders.

There's just one thing holding you back from it.

Paralysis.

You are paralyzed. Perhaps you don't recognize it yet, but we all are. Throughout our lives, we find ourselves in situations that we just can't seem to change. Carrying burdens too heavy for too long. Living broken lives that leave us stuck.

Perhaps it's moving on from something in your past, changing a bad behavior, or repairing a relationship. Maybe it's overcoming addiction, making different choices, or improving your health. Whatever the paralysis is, it is a burden in your life that you are not intended to carry.

And it's holding you back from the future that God has planned for you.

You see, his future for you relies on you not remaining paralyzed. It relies on you finding faith so strong it helps you scale that mountain you never thought possible. It relies on overcoming fears so great you would rather run away than face them. And it relies on you trusting God blindly to take the steps down the paths that he *needs* you to take.

You've already taken the first step. And I'm going to congratulate you on it. You picked up this book.

You. Are. Ready.

I've stood where you've stood. Oh, man, have I. And I know I will again. And again.

I've stared impossible feats in the face and had possible take its place. I've had trembling anxiety replaced with an instantaneous, unexplainable peace. I've had resounding disbelief replaced with such a tremendous amount of blind faith that it changed the entire course of my life.

I had my planned-out future crumble and fall way to reveal the most shocking, beautiful mission in life I could have ever imagined. Dreams I never knew I had bubbled to the surface and burst like a geyser. My life turned completely upside down, but somehow, finally felt right side up.

It blew my socks off.

This all happened because God rehabilitated my life. He restored my faith and trust. He repurposed my view on life. And he created my recovery.

He's ready to do the same for you. His rehabilitation clinic is open for business, and you have a reserved one-on-one appointment. He's ready to guide you. He's ready to heal you. And he's ready to help you move.

Welcome to *The Paralyzed Movement.*

WHAT GOD HAS
REVEALED

Impossible Is Impossible

Jesus said, "I will come and heal ~~him~~ her."

Matthew 8:7

Before you jump on me about editing God's word above, please pause to think what Jesus would think of this edit. I believe Jesus would be all for it. And that's why I did it. He was, after all, an equal opportunity healer. He never discriminated based on gender. Jesus healed men *and* women. So, please, work with me here and follow to see where I am taking you with this. It's important.

If you ask me, women need to hear this message from God. We all need to hear that Jesus wants to heal us. We are typically so focused on everyone else, we don't prioritize thinking about our own issues. We are so consumed with keeping our lives together and in order, we don't have time to invest in overcoming what doesn't make us feel well. We are so heavily burdened, we simply don't have the energy to figure our crap out.

We are paralyzed. Unable to move. Fearful to change. Bound to despair.

Sounds purely pitiful, doesn't it?

When Jesus said, "I will come and heal him" (Matthew 8:7), he wasn't just talking about the paralyzed man that he was getting ready to heal; he was talking about you. He wasn't just preempting the miracle he was about to perform; he was using the moment as a metaphor for the miracle he wants to perform in your life.

You are paralyzed. You have this impossible, overwhelming, crippling issue that you have tried and tried to overcome, but you just keep failing and failing. Jesus says to you, "I will come and heal you."

You have given up, thrown in the towel, and lost all hope that there is any possibility to break the chains of the burden you are carrying. It would take a miracle, you say. Jesus says to you, "I *am* your miracle."

In fact, the definition of a miracle is "an extraordinary event manifesting *divine* intervention in human affairs."

Please note, the definition does not say, "an extraordinary event manifesting *your* intervention in human affairs."

It also doesn't say, "an extraordinary event manifesting *somebody else's* intervention in human affairs."

No, it doesn't.

It says, "divine intervention." To be divine is to be like God. And guess what? We aren't God. There's just one powerful, amazing God in charge, and that is God the Father.

What that means is, if we need a miracle in the areas in our lives where we are paralyzed, we are simply not going to get it without God's intervention.

The truth is that God can perform a miracle in your life. And he has a big reason to do so. He has great plans for every one of us and doesn't want anything paralyzing us or holding us back from those plans.

But the fact is that Satan will do everything he can to stop us from living the life that God intends for us. Whatever your struggle is, Satan will give us every reason to be complacent. He is, as I like to say, a big ol' meanie! He is the ultimate destroyer. He will lie like a rug, make us fearful to move, and do anything in his power to paralyze us from God's will for our lives.

But Satan's power is not God's power. When we have accepted Jesus Christ as our Lord and Savior, God's power within us allows us to push aside Satan's hold on us. We get to flick Satan off our shoulders, and we get the courage to continue walking down the path God has created for us.

Our paralysis can be rehabilitated! God can overcome what we deem as impossible and perform miracles in our own lives! *Impossible is impossible* when we have Jesus in our lives! Yes, you read that right. I said impossible is *impossible*.

I know, I know. This is so in contrast to what we've been brought up hearing and believing. I can hear you saying it now, "Impossible is possible, woman!" But Jesus himself poked a hole in this familiar phrase. Jesus looked at them intently and said,

*"Humanly speaking, it is impossible.
But with God everything is possible."*
Matthew 19:26

In this verse, Jesus is saying that *everything* is possible with him in the picture. So, if that's the case, "impossible" isn't even a possibility. *Impossible is impossible* says that very thing! The phrase "impossible is possible" doesn't work because it actually gives room for impossibilities to exist. And with God in the picture, it's clear that's not truth.

In fact, think about the gravity of what Jesus is saying in this verse right before he tells us that everything is possible, "Jesus looked at them intently and said, 'Humanly speaking, it is impossible.'" Yes, it's true, the word "impossible" was a word invented by humans. He's completely dismissed this word in this Scripture. It's *our* word, not his. He's flat out saying that with him in the picture, *everything* is possible. Doesn't that mean the word "impossible" should cease to exist? Shouldn't we dismiss it as a word in our vocabulary? It's not in his! The word impossible *is* impossible through the eyes of God.

Why am I harping? Because I know that impossible exists right now in your life. There are things that you think you simply can't overcome, can't change, can't achieve. Or maybe you feel that someone that you love is dealing with a situation that is impossible for them to ever overcome. In some way, shape, or form, "impossible" and all the hopelessness that it brings, exists in your life right now.

It's time to change that mindset.

Someone who chose the mindset to overcome the impossible was Christopher Reeve. If you are old enough, you will remember him as the actor who played Superman in the 1980s. He was simply the best Superman that was ever cast. Handsome and heroic.

Tragically, in 1995 Christopher was in an equestrian accident that resulted in a spinal cord injury that left him paralyzed from the shoulders down. To understand the gravity of the injury, he suffered from what some call a hangman injury and was 1/16 of an inch from dying. He was told he had no chance of moving below the shoulders ever again.

But in typical Superman fashion, Christopher Reeve accepted none of it. He refused to accept impossible as his reality; his mindset was the opposite. He was going to move again despite doctor after doctor telling him, "What you want to achieve is impossible."

And he did it. He proved them all wrong. Christopher was able to make snow angel movements in the water. He was able to push off the pool with his feet. He was able to make hand gestures! Superman didn't just accept his situation and exist in it. He didn't wallow in a sea of self-pity. No! He believed in his opportunity to be healed, and he set his mind to it.

The following quote of his continues to be an all-time favorite of mine:

"So many of our dreams at first seem impossible, then they seem improbable, and then, when we summon the will, they soon become inevitable."

—Christopher Reeve

Go ahead, read that again please.

How does that quote resonate with you? I can tell you that it literally gives me chills. It could not be any closer to the truth.

Christopher Reeve was also quoted as saying the following:

"Every scientist should remove the word 'impossible' from their lexicon."

—Christopher Reeve

Replace the word "scientist" with "person," and you have what God wants so badly for us to do: remove the word "impossible" from our lexicon. When we summon the will, *everything is possible.* That's the truth God wants us to hang onto. The miracles in our lives are just waiting to unfold.

So how about it? Are you ready to believe in your miracle? After all, God doesn't reserve miracles for only those who are physically unwell. So, we can't either! God has been performing mental miracles in the lives of humans since the beginning of time. There are countless stories of people whose faith in God has helped them to overcome the greatest obstacles and burdens in their lives. And your story is next.

Healed and Revealed

The subject of miracles is one that I happen to know well, and not because I did some research for this book, but because I witnessed it first-hand.

It was not until I heard the retired officer, who was the first at the scene, speak to the 911 operator that I knew it was severe. My fiancé, Todd, was lying in a ditch after a horrible accident on a four-wheeler. He and his daughter, Eliana, had been traveling home down the gravel road when a deer darted out in front of them and decided to steer them off course.

To prevent them from hitting the deer, Todd locked up the brakes causing the four-wheeler to fishtail out of control. In an attempt to keep his daughter from flying off onto the hard gravel, Todd decided to divert into the ditch to cushion any fall. Only, he was not aware of the hidden ramp in the ditch that sent them and the ATV flying, and Todd went face-first into the bank of the ditch.

Eliana, fortunately, suffered only a few bruises and scrapes, although she will stake claim to suffering the emotional scars of the accident. And rightly so, how scary for her! Todd, however, did not fare so well.

As I was in the ditch comforting him, he was alert and talking. He was actually calming us both down. His injuries didn't seem too significant; I thought, perhaps, a broken arm, a broken leg. But then I heard the retired officer who was first on the scene say it:

"We need the bird."

Suddenly, my panic set in. I knew if a life flight helicopter was on its way, we were dealing with a much bigger situation than I had anticipated. As soon as he was in flight and Eliana was safely in her grandparents' care, I headed to the hospital and found myself trembling with fear.

Physically shaking, I began to pray, begging and pleading with God to help Todd. Then I heard it. A promise placed upon my heart. "He will be healed."

And again, I heard, "He will be healed."

Over and over again, God repeated this to me. God knew I was losing my mind. He knew I needed peace.

Well, it worked. God's truth spoke to me, and this strange peace and hope took over and choked out my fears. I was in the midst of the most significant panic of my life, heart pounding, legs shaking, voice rambling, and God just disrupted it. Everything calmed.

Everything.

These peaceful words from God carried on.

Within the next few hours, we learned that Todd had shattered his C6 vertebrae and fractured his C7. His C6 was completely gone. Totally decimated.

Think of the gravity of that. A critical part of your spine completely shattered. The bone fragments were, in fact, scattered throughout his spinal cord. Shortly thereafter, we received the very unfortunate news that Todd, in fact, had a severe spinal cord injury.

He was paralyzed.

These are completely terrifying words for anyone to hear. All I could think about was how Todd's life had completely changed in an instant. He had just been running the bases in a neighborhood kickball game with the kids the night before. Two days before that, we crossed the finish line together after running the last challenge of our body shaping program. And later that night, we were dancing ridiculously in front of our kids to embarrass them.

All that lost in an instant.

I couldn't stop thinking about what was going through his mind. "Will I ever be able to play ball again with my kids?" "Will I be in a wheelchair for the rest of my life?" "Will she want to be with me if I am?" The agony I felt for him was immense.

Then I remembered God's words: "He will be healed." This promise became our beacon of hope.

By day four, Todd still had no movement with his right leg or arm. The night before, he had been in awful discomfort. His body and mind were fighting a battle, and Todd had been trembling terribly for over a day. We were concerned the trembling resulted from the injury, but after monitoring it for a while, doctors shared with me that Todd was suffering from great anxiety.

He was trembling in fear.

This was a type of anxiety I was familiar with. For years, I suffered from anxiety that violently shook my limbs. It was an anxiety filled with hopelessness, fear, and lies from the big ol' meanie and destroyer. Paralyzing anxiety.

But as my faith journey with God progressed, I discovered a weapon against it. A verse that would calm my body and provide me the peace I needed. I shared that verse with Todd.

> *Do not be anxious about anything, but in every situation,*
> *by prayer and petition, with thanksgiving, present your*
> *requests to God. And the peace of God, which transcends*
> *all understanding, will guard your hearts and your minds*
> *in Christ Jesus.*

Philippians 4:6–7 NIV

While Todd had been a lifelong believer in Christ, he had just started the process of truly developing a relationship with him—really getting to know him and his word. Putting trust in him and having blind faith in his plan was not a path he had been down before. That was about to change.

Todd, still trembling, listened to that verse and closed his eyes. Focusing on the verse and God's promise that "He will be healed," Todd started praying.

And he started having blind faith in God's amazing power. Todd gave his anxiety to God. Completely and fully.

After several seconds of Todd praying, Todd's body calmed. His trembling stopped in an instant. It was nuts. The trembling never again returned.

But God's blessings didn't stop there.

Within the next couple of hours, the right side of his body started to wake up. God started with waking up his foot. The next day came his leg. The next day he was a Rockette, kicking his leg at us when we annoyed him. Every day—hold that—every *hour,* something new was happening.

Six days later- Todd was walking assisted with a walker. The following day, he was walking solo with a walker. I'm serious; I'm not lying. Even dancing a little jig. And the following day, he blew our socks off when he decided to stand up next to his bed and dance with no aid at all—to Keith Urban, of course.

We simply could not believe what we were seeing. The impossible was unfolding right before our eyes.

It was miraculous.

Looking back at the videos we took showing this miracle is simply profound. God was at work. And Todd was too: every day waking up with a hopeful attitude and going to God in prayer.

Todd continued to put his trust in God to heal him, and God healed him. This paralyzed, broken-necked, spinal cord injury patient was walking. In fact, Todd's physical therapist said,

"In the thirty-five years I've been doing this,
I've never seen anything like it."

– Peg

God had kept his promise to me: "He will be healed."

Don't get me wrong here. I know that not all physical battles result in this outcome. No one can be certain or reliant on God performing physical miracles. They are a part of his plan and his plan alone.

But what we can be certain of and reliant on is the role that we play in the process. Consider Todd's role in this story. He was not expecting to receive a miracle from God but was also a willing participant in it. He had the right mindset of hope, determination, and hard work. He had blind faith in the work God would do. And he had total and complete trust in God's will.

This leads me to beg the question: Would you do (or have you done) the same if you had a physical battle in your life? If you were battling physical paralysis, what effort would you (or did you) make to overcome it?

Based on the times I've asked this question in my workshops, I rarely come across someone indicating they would give an average or below average effort to overcome physical paralysis. Instead, most people say they would try as hard as they can and for as long as it would take to gain movement in their life.

Now let's change gears. Think about one thing that has been *psychologically* paralyzing you the most and the longest in your life. And I repose the above question to you: that one thing that has been paralyzing you in your life for some time, what effort have you made to overcome it? How long have you been working to overcome it? Take a moment and write down your thoughts.

If you are one of the few that answered this question with the same level of effort as you would a physical battle, well done. Keep working hard, and with God by your side, you will succeed. But for most people, the two answers do not compare. The level of time and effort that is spent on overcoming psychological paralysis is simply not at the same level. The physical effort wins ninety-nine percent of the time.

So why the difference? Why are we willing to work harder and longer to move physically, but the very things that paralyze us psychologically and keep us from happiness, peace, and purpose get our minimum effort?

There are many reasons we could give on why we have not given the same level of effort. We have tossed out our excuses time and time again. In fact, we are becoming masters of justifying our complacency. But all of these excuses have one single thing in common: lies from Satan. These excuses that we give, either to others or to ourselves, come from him and him alone. His mission to destroy us mentally, emotionally, and spiritually is like a heat-seeking missile.

I know that I am a victim of buying into these lies as well. I've struggled for years battling paralysis. I've spent the majority of my life battling control issues and about seventy-five percent of my life trying to overcome anxiety. While I know that as of late, I'm working hard to change these areas of my life, I gave these my minimum effort for a significant portion of my life.

But there have been successes! I am proof that when you give something to God that you think won't change, he can perform a miracle. Impossible is impossible when it comes to God. I will shout this from the mountaintops from now till my final day. If God can transform me, he can transform anything!

For at least thirty years, I was paralyzed with this constant need for me to receive attention from men. This presented itself in many different forms that I've had to overcome, but all ultimately boiling down to one common trait—I felt this overwhelming need to be accepted by men. As I look back, like many women, it was driven by a long history of not feeling acceptance.

For example, when I was growing up, I was a complete and total tomboy. I loved playing in the dirt, catching crawdads and having a bat and ball in my hand. I played more hours of baseball and football in my backyard than I can count. I grew up on a block of boys with the only other girl being my life-long bestie Jenny who was equal to me in the tomboy category. We didn't just play ball with the boys, we felt we were one with them.

So, when it came time to sign up for baseball one year, I was told that I could not play because I was a girl. This devastated me. My parents tried to convince me to play softball, but I was having none of it. I was a baseball player. I was their teammate. I was as good as they were. None of it made sense to me. For the first time in my life, the fact that I was a girl meant that I would not be accepted by the boys.

I think that spurred something in me that would carry through the rest of my life. This little feminist wasn't going to let anyone hold her back from being accepted by men. For example, I hung out with guys throughout high school and college. There's absolutely nothing wrong with that, except that sometimes, as I navigated those years, that acceptance I desired translated into unhealthy behaviors. Some of those behaviors hurt people that I cared about a lot. As I navigated into the real world in a male-dominated industry, the need for acceptance by men transformed into an unhealthy obsession with work and success. It was then that I decided that my mission in life was to succeed in a "man's world." No one was going to stop me.

This may well be the starting point of where my striving to climb the corporate ladder started and my paralyzed life as a workaholic began.

For close to fifteen years, my focus on making bank, making President's Club, and making the 40 Under 40 list took priority over making dinner for my fam. My mission for promotions, leadership roles, and big sales wins shadowed over the time I had to be present in my children's lives. The more I succeeded in work, the more I felt I failed in life.

All the while, my innate desire to be a wonderful mom, wife, and woman was put on hold. My "recipe for success" didn't taste sweet at all.

That was until I got the dream job that was going to "fix it all." I was promised I would make serious bank, travel to nearly every continent, stay in nothing but five-star resorts, and eat at Michelin Star restaurants.

And I did. All of that. I had, as my friends would say, a super sexy dream job.

I had finally found my way to the top of that ladder that I had dreamed of climbing, in the company of all the men I felt destined to be accepted by.

But I was miserable.

Completely miserable.

My heart did not want to be traveling the world. My heart wanted to be home. It wanted family, and it wanted to see my kids grow.

The top of that ladder didn't feel good at all. I had everything I had ever wanted going for me, but the feelings that consumed me were anxiety and pain. I was missing out on being a mom.

But thank God for God!

He showed me that it was possible to for me to live a better way. He started healing my heart and showing me what truly mattered and why he put me on this Earth. He showed me my mission, to help my family, to help others, and to help spread God's truth.

When I started tuning into what God wanted for me in my life, the doors started opening to make it happen. God helped me heal this paralysis in my life, and as a result, I got to get busy being the mom and woman I desired to be.

I had said a lot of prayers over the years for God to rescue me from the upside-down world I felt I was living in. But it wasn't until God got a grip on me that I started to feel what I needed to feel from him. I was totally accepted by God. I was beautiful and successful in his eyes. He was all I needed.

I vividly remember the time when God took the paralysis of being accepted by men from me. Or, should I say, when I gave it to him. After discovering that was no longer the way I wanted to lead my life, I found myself bawling in my car, pounding on my steering wheel, crying out to God, "Thank you for rescuing me from that pit I had been in!" It was like I puked out the drug and finally saw clearly. I no longer needed it; I had God.

God was there to help me walk from this broken area of my life. He healed me! With God's help, I have found freedom. And he hasn't stopped. God continues prove to me that impossible is impossible with him in the picture.

But it's not just my own miracles I've witnessed. Along this ministry journey, I've watched women overcome significant paralyzing battles in their lives.

I met a woman who struggled with social anxiety nearly her whole life, and I got to watch her get out of her comfort zone at church and speak in front of a huge crowd. One woman dealing with a tragic death in her family found a way to see beyond the grief weighing her down and make progress in healing. And I watched a woman that thought she never could pursue her dream job do it.

I could go on and on.

Inside and outside of my speaking journey, there has been story upon story of women who were able to overcome incredible odds because of God's presence in their lives. Now, what about you? Where are you on your journey? Have you turned to God to overcome the things paralyzing you in your life? If not, it's your turn.

Do you know what it is that God wants to heal for you? Do you know the miracle you need him to perform? Do you know what is paralyzing you?

Take a moment to reflect on this and write down what comes to mind. And as we journey through this book, reflect on these areas of your life and journal the truths you discover along the way.

Biblical Meaning

Let's back up and talk about what we really mean when we are talking about being "paralyzed." Paralysis is a super old word. It started well before biblical times. Understanding its origins really helps give insight into the meaning behind it back when Jesus walked the earth.

The word "paralytic" comes from the ancient Greek word, *para*, meaning "from." *Luo,* the second part of the word, means "to loosen, break, destroy, untie, set free, take off, release."

When you look at this definition, I find it interesting that it doesn't describe a state of *physical* paralysis. There is not a reference to the inability to move or being disabled. In fact, the definition, in my opinion, seems to define a state of bondage, which represents being mentally, emotionally, and spiritually paralyzed. For simplicity purposes, I like to call this psychological paralysis.

I'm not suggesting that the word doesn't have physical meaning because it certainly does. The Bible uses the word "paralysis" in both of these contexts when describing people in the Bible who were physically unable to move and psychologically unable to move.

When it comes to this biblical definition, do you see what I see? I visualize someone carrying a burden. Someone who can't free themselves of something. Trapped. Broken. Needing freedom.

Do you see it? Ask yourself, when or where in your life have you felt . . .

Tied down?

Broken?

Destroyed?

Bound?

If I were to venture a guess, a time or place came to mind for you—more than likely more than one time or place. If you are anything like me, a whole crapload of things came to mind! Because sin rules our lives and the lives of the people surrounding us, we are destined to be paralyzed at some stage of our lives. Paralysis is essentially a guaranteed reality for our existence.

We've all carried heavy burdens that affect our ability to move. We've all experienced that feeling of being unable to change unhealthy situations, unresolved pasts, broken relationships, or bad choices in our lives. We've all been made to feel powerless to change. We've all felt too anxious to move. We've all felt stuck.

Ugh, right?

Here's the deal though. Jesus knew we would feel this way. He knew people were experiencing this type of paralysis when he walked the earth. He knew that it would continue for the remainder of our time on Earth.

So, Jesus did what he does. He spoke to us using metaphors, and he performed miracles to heal the paralyzed.

His Empirical Miracles

As some of you likely already know, Jesus was in the business of healing the paralyzed long before my husband. It was one of the many remarkable miracles that he performed during his walk on Earth. In fact, the verse we've been leaning on, "I will come and heal him," (Romans 8:7) were the very words that Jesus uttered about healing the paralyzed servant of a Roman officer.

Read Romans 8:5–13.

To summarize, after a Roman officer asked Jesus for help because his servant was paralyzed and in pain, Jesus offered to go to the officer's house to heal him. But then the Roman officer essentially said, "Yo, Jesus, no need. Your words will do." That move really impressed Jesus. So much so that Jesus told him, "You have the greatest faith I've seen in all of Israel."

So, here's a guy who's not even Jewish and is believed to have never even met Jesus, yet he had this incredible faith in Jesus' ability to heal his servant. Not only that, but he also knew that Jesus' words could heal. His words! Not his touch. Not his presence. Just his words!

And they did! As a result of the Roman officer's blind faith, Jesus rewarded him and healed his servant at that very moment. Jesus' words healed him.

We are going to keep revisiting this story because there is so much meat in it. But I first want to address why this story should be so significant to you.

Here's why.

Because it is about you.

You are the paralyzed servant.

We have discussed the dual meaning of the word "paralyzed." That it has both a physical and a psychological significance. While this miracle demonstrates the power of physical healing, it can be assumed that this healing wasn't just reserved for the physically paralyzed. It was likely intended for a broader paralyzed audience: each and every one of us.

How do we know this?

Because of how Jesus spoke to us.

Throughout the Bible, Jesus used parables to communicate to believers. Parables have been described as "earthly stories with a heavenly meaning." He used parables to communicate to his believers the truths of the kingdom of God.

In other words, Jesus used hidden messages in his words to communicate the truth of God.

As a matter of fact, there are forty-six different parables in the Bible that Jesus used to communicate his truth. These parables are intended to teach us and guide us in our lives.

But Jesus didn't just use parables to communicate hidden messages. He used metaphors too—through his miracles. *Who* he used was an essential metaphoric part of Jesus' ministry.

As is the case when Jesus healed the blind (John 9).

> *Jesus said, "For judgment I came into this world, that*
> *those who do not see may see, and those who see may*
> *become blind."*
>
> ### John 9:39 ESV

When he healed this blind man, He used it as a sign to speak to *all people*. He was telling *all of us* that, while at first, we may not see God's truth or our spiritual blindness clearly, as our faith in Jesus grows, so does our vision of his truth. In return, he is also telling us that those who insist they can see perfectly without Jesus will continue blindly in their life.

Jesus metaphorically used the blind to tell us that we are all blind in life. Then, when we believe in him, the truth becomes visible.

Another example is when Jesus brought his friend Lazarus back from the dead (John 11).

> *Jesus said to her, "I am the one who brings people back to*
> *life, and I am life itself. Those who believe in me will live*
> *even if they die. Everyone who lives and believes in me will*
> *never die. Do you believe that?"*
>
> ### John 11:25–26 GW

Through the miracle of raising Lazarus from the dead, Jesus was showing a sign to *all people*. He was communicating that if we believe in him, we all will have life after death. His planning of this miracle was even documented before Lazarus' death. That's how important it was for him.

Communicating the message of life after death to all of us was a critical mission for Jesus.

Jesus knew that we would all struggle with finding comfort in accepting our death someday. But Jesus was telling us that while we all die, we will live on if we believe in him. He metaphorically used a dead guy to let us know the greatest truth that could have been revealed to us.

And yet, here is another example is Jesus' metaphoric miracle of the hearing and speech impaired (Mark 7).

> *Looking up to heaven, he sighed and said,*
> *"Ephphatha," which means, "Be opened!" Instantly*
> *the man could hear perfectly, and his tongue was freed*
> *so he could speak plainly!*
>
> **Mark 7:34–35**

A deaf man with a speech impediment was brought to Jesus to be healed. Jesus plugged this guy's ears and put his spit on his tongue, and said, "Ephphatha," that is, "Be opened." Jesus did this to *communicate to us* so that our ears would be opened to hearing God's word and our tongues would be used to glorify God.

We all struggle with understanding the truth. But Jesus metaphorically used a deaf and mute man to tell us that when we listen to God's word, we will begin to speak the truth to spread his good message.

So hopefully, you can see where I'm going with this. Jesus used very specific people to reveal his truth to us. This is why we can safely assume that Jesus metaphorically used a paralyzed man to speak directly to us.

Understand me, this paralyzed man was a real person and an actual receiver of Jesus' miracle. Jesus certainly wanted to heal him and perform a miracle to demonstrate his tremendous power. But the paralyzed man was also likely being used by Jesus *metaphorically* to speak to those that are psychologically paralyzed—in other words, each and every one of us.

So, place yourself there. Place yourself in the position of that paralyzed man in the Bible. Look at what he is saying to you. It's a life-changing truth.

Jesus said, "I will come and heal ~~him~~ her."

Matthew 8:7

How does it make you feel to hear that?

He will come and heal you.

Take that to the bank, kids. God wants to heal you from what is paralyzing you. He wants to heal you from what has you living in fear, living in bondage, and keeping you from pursuing your purpose. His mission is dependent on it.

Let me put it differently for you because I'll admit, there is nothing sexy about talking about paralysis. Am I right? In fact, most of us want to run from it. It's too hard. Too tiring. Too threatening. Just too icky to dwell on.

So, how about this instead?

God wants to perform a miracle in your life.

It's true. He does. You are the paralyzed young servant, my friend. He was speaking to you. He's prepared to perform a miracle in your life with the things that paralyze you.

Does that get you excited?

So ask yourself, when you consider God performing a miracle in your life, what is it that immediately comes to mind? And almost as immediately as it comes to mind, do you dismiss it?

That thing.

That thing that has been so overwhelming, it's weighed your entire life down. That thing that you've tried so desperately hard to change, but you can't. That thing that you've had such a desperately tight grip on, you've stopped caring that it's destroying your life.

That thing that, although a thing of the past, is so deeply ingrained in you, you simply can't let it go. That thing that you have dreamed about every day for years but is just too impossible to pursue.

That thing.

That is the miracle that God wants to perform in your life. And he can. And he will.

The Scriptures don't lie, my friends. Everything that keeps you in bondage, he wants to heal. Everything that has you living in fear, he wants to heal. Everything that is keeping you from pursuing his purpose, he wants to heal.

He said to her, "Daughter, your faith has healed you.
Go in peace and be freed from your suffering."

Mark 5:34 NIV

Let me just shake you one more time to make sure this is getting through. God does not want you to remain paralyzed. He wants you to be freed, and he wants you to find peace. For that one thing that you've determined is too possible to overcome, God wants to perform a miracle in your life.

There are no ifs, ands, or buts about this. It's imperative that he performs the miracle because this is where spiritual growth comes from. This is how he produces fruitful, faithful believers. This is how he reveals himself to us. And most importantly, this is how he frees us to pursue his will and the purpose that he has for our lives. All he needs from us is to be willing participants.

I'm ready, are you?

Hallelujah!

Revealing Questions

A miracle is in your future. Can't you feel it?! But to get that started, there is work for you to do with God. Take some time to reflect on these important topics from this chapter.

1. Impossible is Impossible

What are you dealing with in your life right now that you've determined is impossible to overcome? Who have you given up on because you view their burdens are impossible to overcome? How hard are you working to overcome those things? How long have you been working to overcome them? Ponder how God can help you change your perspective and navigate these areas in your life differently.

2. Miracles

What miracles have you seen transpire in your life or in the lives of others? In the areas that you are feeling paralyzed or in the life of someone you love that is paralyzed, what would a miracle look like for you? Have you put your faith and trust in God that he can help you heal? Does the healing of the paralyzed give you hope for change?

3. Metaphors

How does it feel to know that God so carefully crafted *who* he healed so it would show you how he wants to heal you? What does it mean to you to know that Jesus' words alone can heal? What's the one thing you are psychologically battling that you want Jesus to heal? How can you spend more time in God's word to help you to heal?

Let Go and Let's Go

Is it easier to say "Your sins are forgiven,"
or "Stand up and walk"?

Matthew 9:5

The other day, I was walking our gravel road, climbing one of the monstrous hills that kicks my butt. A never-ending, butt-burning, lung-failing hill. The whole time I was suffering up that hill, I was focused on the other side of it. The moment the trial would ease up, I could catch my breath and finally coast. I could not wait to get there, and I was doing all I could to not live in the pain of the moment. I was focused on the glorious end of it.

That's when it dawned on me that perhaps we also need to navigate our lives with this same perspective.

I don't know how many struggle hills I've climbed in my life, figuratively speaking, but it's countless. I'm sure you can say the same. And if I were to venture a guess, I think it's safe to say that some of those challenges in our lives would be better described as mountains.

Those never-ending, moral-burning, life-is-failing challenges. Those "why is God letting this happen?" moments. I know you relate here. . . . You have your list. It's equally as vast. Those hills and mountains we have climbed have been engrained in our memories for the rest of our earthly existence.

Rarely, amid my most significant life challenges was I focused on what was really awaiting me on the other side—the downhill side. You know, the side when the trial would finally ease up. When I would be able to catch my breath. When I could start coasting through life again.

Instead, in almost every instance, I was focused on the torture of what I was enduring. The hopelessness of it never ending. And the exhaustion from the battle.

We can all find ourselves in this trap. Let's admit it. It is so hard to be Jack Handy amid our hell on Earth. Being all positive in the midst of our negativity is just not our thang. It cramps our wah-wah lifestyle to have hope, faith, and trust in a better tomorrow.

If I'm offending you by saying that, I'm sorry, but the truth is, we human folk can really lap up misery. We like to bathe in it. Swim in it. Drown in it.

Until, that is, our perspective changes. Or should I say, until he changes our perspective.

The only moments of trial that I recall being focused on cresting the mountain, being hopeful of the peace beyond it, and trusting that I would overcome the challenge were the trials in which I was close to God. Of course, one of those trials was Todd's accident. I remember vividly when God laid "He will be healed" on my heart on the way to the hospital. And when he subsequently repeated that to me over and over again.

This was a life-changing perspective to gain. Instead of focusing on the reality that was visibly in front of us, which was grim, painful, and never ending, we were focused on the end game: Todd being healed.

Honestly, it made our journey unbelievable. I look back at it and am in disbelief at how much fun we had while going through hell! Seriously. We did so much celebrating, laughing, singing, dancing, and praising along the way. It really is nutso to think about.

God changed our perspective. We believe this not only changed the experience of the journey, but it also changed the outcome. God needed us to be positive so Todd could work hard and get stronger in the only window he had. If we had ignored God's message and lapped up the sea of misery and negativity instead, there is no doubt that Todd would have missed his window of recovery.

This leads me to urge you to check where you are. If you are in the midst of a climb, where is your perspective focused? Are you focused on the other side? Are you asking God for help? Or are you wallowing in self-pity?

I don't want to come across as insensitive. Girl, I'm with you—I know it's not easy. I know the pain. I know the hopelessness. But having hope that you can "let go and let God" can help you overcome. Having faith in the peace that follows and being continuously present with him during the journey is the least painful way to navigate your way up that hill.

To give you some perspective, every year in Iowa, there is a bike ride across the entire state of Iowa called RAGBRAI. It starts at the Missouri River on one hot Saturday in July and ends at the Mississippi River on the following hot Saturday in July. All the days in between are hot. On average, 468 miles of hot. And 468 miles of hills. And when I say hills, I mean *hills*. The climb over the week averages 14,730 feet, which is essentially the same height as Mount Rainier in Washington. On this hot week in July, nearly 20,000 crazy people essentially ride their bikes up a mountain.

I was one of those crazy people—sort of—twice.

In 2009, I did a forty-five-mile, 2,182-foot climb of RAGBRAI. I did RAGBRAI all sorts of wrong though. I did not train. In fact, I had not been on a bike in years.

And, well, I did it on a beach cruiser.

Yep. You heard me right, a beach cruiser. No one told me that I shouldn't!

If you aren't a biker and don't understand the challenge of this, a beach cruiser is a heavy bike intended for riding on a beach. Flat ground, my friends. It is not designed for hills of any height.

You see where I am going here.

While other people were flying past me, I was on my beach cruiser, going 0.5 miles per hour trying to get up these hills. It was grueling, painful, exhausting, and miserable. Because I was so behind schedule (I left at eight a.m. and didn't complete the leg until eight p.m., if that gives you an idea), I did not get to stop at any of the fun stops along the way, which was really the whole reason I decided to do RAGBRAI anyway.

In short, I had zero fun, was totally miserable, and almost bailed into the sagging wagon. (The only thing between me and that wagon was my stubborn nature.) RAGBRAI 2009 was hell on Earth. Never again.

Until I did do it again.

This time in 2011. I was smarter this time and had borrowed a friend's road bike. And oh, what a difference it made!

I was like a gazelle on wheels, swiftly and smoothly navigating those hills. While it was still a challenge, I was smiling, laughing, singing, and sailing through the day. I even had ample time to stop and enjoy all the fun stops. RAGBRAI 2011 went down as a success.

Chicas, let me tell you, choosing to let go and let God be on your side as you navigate the hills in your life is the same thing. He is the road bike. He will take a painful challenge and make it easier so you can sail through it. He will give you moments in the midst to still enjoy life and find happiness in the trial. And he will get you to the top swifter and smoother than you could do alone.

So, ask yourself, which bike you are on now? Are you on the beach cruiser, or are you on the road bike?

I know the difference in my scenario is that I chose to do this challenge, but I also chose to make that challenge more manageable. I knew what I was doing wasn't working for me. It was not effective, and it was painful, so I made a change.

If we want our trials to get easier, we have to make a change too. We have to equip ourselves with God. He will make our uphill easier and get us to our downhill sooner. Now, who doesn't want that?

As you navigate the hill you are climbing, or one that is just around the corner, navigate it with God and keep your focus on what's on the other side. There has never been a hill that didn't have another, easier downhill side. Eventually, you will get to coast and rest.

Rise Up and Walk

Jesus' walk on Earth was filled with helping people during their most difficult climbs in life. The people he healed were able to see beyond their difficult journey and have hope that Jesus would take them to the other side. A great example of this was the paralyzed man in Capernaum.

Read Mark 2:1–12.

To summarize the story, a man who had been paralyzed his whole life was carried by four men on a mat to meet Jesus to be healed.

People were pouring out of the home to see Jesus perform miracles. The men carrying the paralyzed man did not want anything standing in their way of getting to Jesus. So, they dug a hole in the roof above Jesus and lowered the man in front of him. In this moment, Jesus was super impressed with the faith of all of them. He said to the paralyzed man,

"My child, your sins are forgiven."

Mark 2:5

Well, this sure ticked off the religious teachers and Pharisees in the audience. Only God could forgive sins. How dare he! Jesus sensed them thinking blasphemy and responded with this:

"Why do you question this in your hearts? Is it easier to say to the paralyzed man, 'Your sins are forgiven,' or 'Stand up, pick up your mat, and walk'? So, I will prove to you that the Son of Man has the authority on earth to forgive sins."

Mark 2:8–10

It was then that Jesus said to the paralyzed man, "Stand up, pick up your mat, and go home!" and immediately after, the man jumped up, grabbed his mat, and walked out.

As you can imagine, the crowd was shocked. Everyone was in awe and said, "We've never seen anything like this before." Rightly so.

First, let me tell you, this story is packed full of so much in its tiny little self. Only twelve verses long, this story unpacks perhaps the greatest truths that Jesus revealed during his walk on Earth. The metaphor master struck again.

Let's first state the obvious. This miracle was, of course, another demonstration of Jesus' remarkable ability to heal. To perform a miracle. To show that *impossible is impossible* with his presence in the picture.

But Jesus used this healing as an opportunity to reveal so much more.

And what he had to reveal was *huge*.

Jesus used the healing of a paralyzed man to prove that he had the power to forgive sins.

Ponder this. At this point in Jesus' miracle tour, he had proven that he had miraculous abilities, but he had not come out and insinuated, "I am God." In fact, he had been trying to keep it under wraps on several occasions. But this moment was different. Jesus was ready for the mic drop.

The significance of Jesus claiming that he had the power to forgive sins was enormous. In the eyes of Jewish leaders in the crowd, Jesus was taking a significant risk by revealing his ability to forgive sins, as it was considered blasphemy. The Jewish leaders believed that Jesus was claiming he could do something that only God could do, which, according to the law at that time, was a mortal sin punishable by death. Jesus was taking a grave risk. And he knew it.

I mean, stop to think about how significant that moment in Jesus' life was. Jesus *knew* the risk. He *knew* he would be persecuted. He *knew* he was putting his life on the line. But it didn't matter to Jesus because that moment in time had to happen during his walk on Earth. He had to put it all on the line to claim to the crowd who he really was. He had to reveal to everyone that he was our path to forgiveness. He had to demonstrate that his forgiveness is what leads to our ability to walk again.

Just look at how Jesus broke this down for us.

> *"Is it easier to say to the paralyzed man, 'Your sins are forgiven,' or 'Stand up, pick up your mat, and walk'?"*
>
> ### Mark 2:8–10

In the Bible, the Greek word translating to forgiveness literally means "to let go." Jesus was telling the crowd and the paralyzed man his sins has been "let go." He's been freed of it. He was no longer chained, bound, confined, or broken by it.

So, you may ask, why did Jesus tell a paralyzed man that his sins had been let go? That he had been forgiven? What did that have to do with healing his paralysis?

Jesus connects forgiveness to healing. He connects forgiveness to rising up and making spiritual progress. He demonstrates that "letting go" equates to moving forward.

Here's the key lesson: We, again, are the paralyzed man. When Jesus died on the cross and forgave us for our sins, he healed us. We've been freed from our sins. We are no longer chained, bound, confined, or broken by it. It has been let go. He's saying you've been released. There's no resentment. You don't owe him or anyone else anything. You don't have to feel shame. You don't have to wallow in your pity party. You just have to *walk*.

Think about the word "walk." What does it insinuate?

It means he doesn't want you to stay in the same broken place. He doesn't want you stuck and unable to move forward. He doesn't want everyone else carrying you for the rest of your life. He wants you walking.

Walking.

Throughout the Bible, the term "walking" is used to refer to spiritual progress. In fact, Paul demonstrated the metaphoric use of this word when he wrote to the Galatians about finding freedom in Christ.

> *So I say, walk by the Spirit, and you will not*
> *gratify the desires of the flesh.*
>
> **Galatians 5:16 NIV**

I know there is something in your life right now that you don't feel capable of walking away from. That you don't feel capable of receiving forgiveness for. Or that you don't feel capable of being able to forgive.

Jesus is telling you in this story, "my child," I can free you from this. "My child," I forgive you for this. "My child, *walk*."

You are his child. HIS CHILD! There is nothing that you have done, can do, or will ever do that will separate you from him. He has not put you in the naughty corner for life. He's freed you from it.

What is it that you have not been able to free yourself from? What is it that you need to release? What is it that you need to let go of?

Jesus says to you, "My child, it's been 'let go' for you already! Stand up and walk!" Join the movement, girl!

Let go and let's go!

Willing Participants

There was a time when I was in a really, really crappy place in life. So sucky that I couldn't even find enjoyment in the fact that my job had taken me to Puerta Vallarta. That sucky.

I set out on a walk down the beach while I was there to do some serious soul-searching about what the heck I was going to do about my life. A life that I was living for the outside world, while ignoring the very soul inside me. A life that should have been a smooth race, but in reality, was a giant butt-kicking. A life that was spinning out of control. A life that was *paralyzed.*

That day on the beach, I set out to seek answers from God. I needed to hear from him. I needed his direction.

As I approached a pier, I came across a woman holding her young toddler by both hands, helping her navigate the waves. The little girl would hold her mom's hands, dip her little butt into the water, pop back up, and then repeat.

I stood there watching them for some time. After a bit, the girl started to let go of her mom's hands and navigate the waves independently. When the waves proved to be too big of a challenge, the little girl would run up the beach to get away, only to realize she was walking alone. You could almost see this realization as she stopped dead in her tracks to turn around and find her mom following right behind her.

That's when it started to sink in with me. I was nearly drowning in my life. I was running straight into rough waves of life, trying to navigate them all on my own. Only I wasn't stopping in my tracks to turn and look to my

Father for help. With the most significant stuff, I wasn't turning to him at all. I didn't want to hear what he had to say.

I was too afraid. Afraid of the journey it would take to overcome. Afraid of living a life without. Afraid of what was on the other side. I was paralyzed with fear.

I had approached overcoming this paralysis in all the wrong ways, spending years of my entire life trying to navigate the world alone. I tried to control every possible thing to ensure that my life did not spin out of control, only to achieve the opposite result. Anxiety. Irrational Fears. Doomsday. All compasses for my every day. Only the compasses had led me down the wrong path.

The path of control.

This path of control had led me to a life that was, well, completely freaking out of control.

- I was paralyzed with codependency and, subsequently, tried to control everything around me only to have that control exacerbate it all.
- I was paralyzed with financial stress, and despite my efforts to control that through furthering my career, our debt was spiraling out of control.
- I was paralyzed with the desire to succeed, and when I controlled the direction my career should take, I just fell further and further away from the life that God wanted me to lead as a mom, wife, and child of God.

As I was standing on the beach pondering whether God would even want to save me from this mess that I had created, the little girl came within my vision once again. This time, she ran away from her mom and took her adorable new floppy hat from the top of her head and chucked it on the ground. The mom immediately rushed over, picked up the hat, and started brushing off the sand. But since it was wet, some of the sand just wouldn't come off. Regardless, the mom just gave her girl a squeeze, plopped that hat back on her head, and sweetly patted her on the butt.

That's when I saw it. It was the perfect picture of what our relationship with God looks like. We trot along happy as a clam with him, then choose to be defiant, run from him, and end up with scum all over us.

We are so naughty! We do this all the time. We really do need a spankin'!

That's where I was at in my journey. I knew I needed God but chose to be defiant and in command instead. What about you? What are the areas in your life where you are defiant?

- Is there someone in your past that you are refusing to forgive?
- Do you find yourself lying, even about the stupidest stuff?
- Is there a person in your life that you just can't stand and gossip about all the time?
- Do you have mean habits in your life that are making you unbearable for others to live with?
- Are you wigging out on a colleague because they aren't meeting your standards?

The list of defiant questions could go on and on and on.

Here's what we need to lay at our feet though: What happens every time we choose to be defiant? What happens when we sin? Of course, we experience pain and consequences, but what else happens?

He forgives us!

God helps us plop that hat back on our heads and dive back in. And he does this with the scum still stuck to us! Our God loves us despite our scum. Despite our imperfections. He is always ready to give us a big hug and a sweet pat on the butt to continue on.

If only we could see God in this gentle, loving way regularly. Do you think we would be more willing to take our scum to him? If we could continually imagine God chasing us into the waves, do you think we'd be more likely to turn to him for help?

There is often this misconception that God will rescue us from anything wrong happening in our lives. Almost that it's his duty and responsibility.

Like a "Yo, God, I screwed up, fix this" mentality. That's not the way he rolls.

God wants to use our troublesome, paralyzed places in life to grow our faith. To make spiritual progress. To walk with his spirit. But to do that, there is one key component that is absolutely necessary.

We have to be a willing participant.

I mean, think back to the story of the paralyzed man in Capernaum. If the paralyzed man didn't believe Jesus and tried to walk on his own, he would have never ventured off his mat. He'd still be paralyzed. Am I right? His circumstances wouldn't have changed one bit. Zilch.

But when he had faith, that all changed.

> *When Jesus saw their faith, he said to the paralyzed man,*
> *"Son, your sins are forgiven."*
>
> **Mark 2:5 NIV**

The paralyzed man's willingness to participate changed everything for him. His *faith* was all that it took. Jesus forgave him in an instant.

And here is the key message I cannot scream loud enough for you to hear:

Jesus' forgiveness of the man's sins was the miracle.

Plain and simple. Jesus' forgiveness made this man walk again. Jesus' forgiveness allowed him to overcome the impossible. Jesus' forgiveness broke him from the bondage that was preventing him from walking.

The paralyzed man's walk was all about forgiveness.

And yes. This willing participant walked. Simply amazing.

For God to perform the miracles we need to overcome the paralysis in our lives, we have to be willing participants. We can't just be lying on our mats waiting expectantly. We have to show God the faith we have in his ability to heal us.

We have to show up ready to give our paralysis to him, even if it means we need the people we love to help us get there. We have to be willing to do whatever it takes to find him, even if it means budging in front of a crowd and digging a hole in a roof to do it. We have to be willing to stand up and walk when God tells us to.

It's incredible what transpired when I finally became a willing participant—when I finally gave it all to God and trusted him to help me overcome what had me paralyzed. It wasn't an easy journey. Having faith can feel damn near impossible sometimes. But he did not fail me. He led me to the other side. He healed me.

He's ready to do the same for you. There is nothing too big or too small he can't tackle for you. "Ain't no valley too low. Ain't no mountain too high." He has it covered. He just needs a willing participant.

And one who's willing to *let go*.

Let Go

God is saying to you, "Let go and let's go." Let go of the things that are paralyzing you and let's get walking. Let's get moving. Pick up your mat, girl, let's roll.

There's just one more critical factor I need to drill on.

In order to move again, it's not just God that needs to let go of the things that are holding us in bondage. It's us. We need to learn to let go too. If God can forgive us, then we should be able to forgive ourselves too. And this is the hardest part.

God knows this about you, so sometimes he tries to convince us in amazing, profound ways. And he did so in a big way with me *for you*.

Let me explain.

Not many people know that when one writes a book, it doesn't necessarily happen in order. In other words, one doesn't necessarily write it from front to back. That has certainly been the case with mine. In fact, a week and a half ago, I was crying and ready to quit because I had so many holes left in the book to write. This devastated me because after five years of muddying my way through this book, I had decided to establish a deadline for finishing the book, but it wasn't looking like I would reach it. In my mind, there was no budging on the deadline. I needed to get it done. For me and for God, it needed to get done. But in that moment, I was so overwhelmed and lost within my own book that I did not think it would happen.

In the midst of a hardcore panic session with God, he laid on my heart, "It will be done." That was a game changer for me.

Well, today, girls, is the last day. This is the day that I get to say, "It is finished." My book will be done. And get this: today is not only deadline day, it also happens to be Good Friday. I had not planned for deadline day to be the same day that Jesus Christ hung dying on the cross for us, uttering the very same words "It is finished" (John 19:30). His last words.

When Jesus had tasted it, he said, "It is finished!"
Then he bowed his head and gave up his spirit.

John 19:30

I do not think it is a coincidence that God waited for today for me to write about forgiveness. Here we are on the very same day that he died on the cross so that we could be forgiven for our sins.

I'm emotional right now. I'm not going to lie.

I just want to shout this louder than anything I have ever shouted in my life. Girls, he took your paralyzing burdens to the cross and died for them. He died for them so that you wouldn't have to carry them anymore! He died for them so that you would be able to find eternal life with him.

I want you to think about what you are refusing to let go of.

And now, picture Jesus, nailed to the cross, his body bloody, tortured. Our King bearing a crown of pain, hanging lifeless. Pause and picture this please.

All of this for *your* forgiveness. All of this for *you*.

When Jesus said, "It is finished," he was saying, "Let go, I have forgiven you. Now you have to forgive yourself. Let go, I have forgiven others. Now you have to forgive them too."

So now I ask you to please go pray. Please go ask Jesus to help you "let go." To help you forgive. To help you walk.

Revealing Questions

As you navigate letting go of the things paralyzing you, take some time to reflect on each of these stages of your journey.

1. Trials

When you are navigating the difficult trials in your life, do you find yourself focused on the misery of the journey, or are you focused on the other side of it? When you think about God helping you navigate that trial, does it ease up the challenges? What is the best way for you to engage God to help find hope during those difficult journeys?

2. Walking

How does it make you feel to have God call you his child? When you hear that God forgives the sins in your life, does that provide you hope? How do these things help you in your spiritual walk? What are ways that you can be proactive with your spiritual growth?

3. Willing Participant

Have you decided to be a willing participant in your healing journey? Are there still things holding you back from having faith that God can help you overcome? What do you need to let go of to make progress in your journey of overcoming? How can God help you through that process?

The Biblical Physical

"For I hold you by your right hand—
I, the Lord your God. And I say to you,
'Don't be afraid. I am here to help you.'"

Isaiah 41:13

I'm gripping something tightly—and I mean tightly. So tightly that my body is suffering and struggling. So tightly, it caused me to have chronic pain. And it is pain that has made me think I'm dying. In fact, it's changed the entire landscape of my physical life. And it's led to me spending gazillions of dollars with doctors trying to find its cause.

That's what's been going on for the past five and half years.

My body is in far contrast from where it was three days before Todd's accident. I shared with you that we had crossed the finish line together as we completed the final test of an extreme body shaping program. In the ten weeks of the program, I managed to lose five inches off my waist, drop two minutes off my mile, and double the number of sit-ups and push-ups I could do in a minute. We were both in the best shape we had been in many years. We were killing it!

Even when Todd was in the hospital, I stayed committed to the maintenance program, attending classes as often as possible. I was intent on leading a healthier, more active life. Nothing else we had going on was going to stop me.

But unfortunately, my commitment to exercise didn't matter. Because my body was in overdrive, and it took a toll.

In the two months that Todd was in the hospital, I somehow managed to

- spend every other full week with Todd at the rehabilitation hospital caring for him,
- work full-time building a business,
- take care of my children and all motherly responsibilities,
- pack up Todd's entire house, including his children's rooms, so they could move into my house when he got out of the hospital (he still needed someone to care for him when he graduated out),
- manage a construction project in my home to prepare my house for Todd's three kids (my stepchildren), and
- plan our wedding.

Yes, a wedding. If Todd and his kids were moving in, we needed to expedite our plan to get hitched. It was what our hearts desired anyway. In fact, truth be told, I officially proposed to Todd the first moment I saw him after surgery. I needed him to know that I wasn't going anywhere, and I wanted to love him for the rest of my life. I tried to convince him there was a chaplain in the hall that could do the deed right then and there, but I guess he wanted to see me in a dress. So, we waited.

But we didn't wait long. Todd and I got married three weeks after he got out of the hospital. Looking back, I'm pretty sure it may be one of the only weddings where people cared more about the groom walking down the aisle than the bride. It was utterly fantastic. And the bonus of it all? We got to share a first dance. My heart is clapping right now.

But wow, those few months. The accident, the moves, the responsibilities, the wedding. I'm not sure how I pulled all of that off. I honestly don't. I scratch my head, trying to figure out where I had time in my day. All I know is that my adrenaline was in full force, off the charts high. It had to have been, right? I had the strength and will of Superwoman. It was surreal.

It would be two weeks following the wedding when that all changed. After finally finding stability, rest, and peace, my body gave up. It was tired.

I woke up one morning with such shoulder pain, I could not lift my arms above my head to wash my hair. I remember having to summon my husband, who still had a paralyzed hand, to help me bathe. Oh my, how the tides had turned.

This continued for a few months and got a little better. But eventually, the pain started to spread, ultimately impacting nearly every part of my body. My back, hips, and groin hurt so bad that it changed my ability to walk normally. I felt, and still feel, like an eighty-year-old woman.

As my body started to go awry, so did my mind. Impending doom crept in. Anxiety ruled my world.

Every doctor visit and test would reveal that nothing was going on. Meanwhile, my pain was convincing me of something entirely different. Certainly, the doctors were missing it. Certainly, I was dying.

My new pain had turned me into a hypochondriac.

This fear of death paralyzed me.

It wasn't until I met with a functional health doctor last year that the truth was revealed.

I was not dying. My body was just not letting go.

It wasn't letting go of the trauma of Todd's accident. It wasn't letting go of the pain from my divorce years ago. It wasn't letting go of my fears. It wasn't letting go of my anxiety. It was just hanging on to it all.

This was verified through actual lab results. My labs indicated stress hormone levels were off in my body. My fight or flight balance in my body was way off course. Although my battle was over, my body was still fighting.

The only solution?

Letting go.

You've probably heard that stress can cause physical problems in the body. It is known to tense muscles. It's known to affect cortisol and adrenaline levels. It's known to cause inflammation and pain over time.

These are the results of not letting go.

What about you? Are you holding on to something that could cause you pain? Are you already experiencing that pain?

Pain is just one example of what the stress of being psychologically paralyzed causes. There are other unfortunate outcomes associated with paralysis such as anger, grief, sadness, resentment, fear, guilt, depression, and anxiety—just to name a few. As our stress builds up from the things paralyzing us, so do our negative emotions and physical issues.

This is no way to live, girls.

Do you relate to these stressors? Is there an area in your life you've identified that paralyzes you and you want to change? It doesn't matter the gravity of the situation—big issues or even what may seem like small issues can cause significant amounts of stress. Perhaps,

- you're stuck at your corporate job, and you just want the courage to chase your dream. Is it keeping you up at night? Are you so fatigued you can barely get through your day?
- you're an addict who's been struggling, and you want to quit instead of having "just one more." Is it affecting your loved ones significantly? Do you feel so much guilt you can hardly stand to face another day?
- you're in a broken relationship, and you know you need to leave but are too afraid. Is it causing you so much anger that you are taking it out on all the wrong people?

This list could go on and on and on, girls. I know this. Everyone has something in their life that is causing stress. Or that makes one feel hopeless. Something that you think, no matter what you do, it's not going to change. Something that seems impossible to ever overcome. But rest assured, you don't have to feel this way forever.

We've heard from God; it's time to let go. Let's tune into that heavily, ladies. Our focus has to change. We need to focus on feeling confident in what God wants for us and start working toward that. We can't continue believing the things in our lives causing negative emotions and pain are here to stay. It's the last thing God wants us to believe.

We have to change our mindset.

Paralyzed Inspiration

Think about the situation people with physical paralysis are in. One might think that they would have every reason to believe their ability to move again is impossible. They have something scientifically preventing them from moving. But that does not change their hope. It doesn't change their fight. And it doesn't change their outcome.

It's because of their mindset.

A great example of this mentality is Ben, who was a patient at the same rehabilitation hospital as Todd. Ben had suffered almost an identical accident to Todd at about the same time.

By the time we met him, he was paralyzed and had no movement in his legs. Todd, at this point, was already walking again. From our perspectives, Ben's chances at walking again looked grim.

I vividly remember watching him in the rehabilitation room. Everything he did required him to use his arms and crawl. I recall Todd and I both feeling this tremendous amount of guilt that Todd had so much, and he had so little. The future we viewed for him was heartbreaking.

But our mentality was not Ben's mentality. He was a God dude. And he had complete and total faith in God. He had this tremendous believer support network coming to cheer him on. His posse would travel in big groups for three hours to just surround him, encourage him, and pray for him. The enthusiasm and positivity were in full force. It was beyond inspirational.

Even so, we had nothing but heaviness in our hearts while they were focused on Ben overcoming the impossible.

We hoped and prayed for progress for him, but ultimately in our hearts, we viewed it as an impossibility that he would ever be able to walk again. The improvement was just not happening. There was no way.

So, imagine our surprise when we saw a video post from the hospital a few months later of Ben walking out of that hospital.

Ben was kicking butt and taking names. No one was holding him back. It was a giant weeping fest for Todd and me to see this if you can imagine. Weeping for joy for Ben and his new future. And weeping in amazement at the tremendous power of God.

Dang it, I'm crying again. It's so overwhelming to relive this moment again.

People dealing with physical battles fight like this all the time. They have hope. They fight. They walk!

And when people have a supportive community cheering them on, it is icing on the cake. They have courage! They have inspiration! They walk!

But Ben wasn't done yet. He didn't just walk, he ran—literally started running again. And even after a setback due to a disc issue where he lost his ability to use his left leg, he still didn't lose hope. He fought back and ran again!

This dude is simply incredible.

And he's the perfect example of how we should be with anything that is paralyzing us. We need to instill that same hope and fight in us. We need to believe that whatever it is in your life that you deem impossible is actually possible with God.

Let's Get Physical

Ben's journey, Todd's journey, and my own journey are all great examples of the focus we have on our physical bodies. We go to great lengths to heal our bodies. Think about the amount of time and money that is spent every year on medical research. On medical care. On pharmaceuticals. And for what? To preserve our bodies to lead mentally unhealthy lives?

We simply can't stop at caring for only our physical well-being. We have to heal our mental well-being as well.

One of the most significant metaphoric examples of how we begin to heal our mental state is by examining our physical bodies themselves. So, I'd like to nerd out here for a minute.

I don't know about you, but when I think about what I learned back in high school, very little stuck with me. I'm sure it served the purpose of training my brain, but I don't believe I retained much from an information standpoint.

I can say, however, that I do recall the lessons we received on how the body works. So, here are the cliff notes for you.

1. The heart is the life center of your body and acts as the engine.
2. The brain is the command center of your body and receives and transmits signals.
3. The spinal cord is the communication system that communicates the signals from the brain to the appropriate nerves.
4. The nerves initiate body movement.

Easy peasy lemon squeezy, right?

So, when someone is unable to physically move, one of the following is happening:

1. Their heart is blocked and unable to work appropriately or not beating well or at all.
2. Nerves in the brain are damaged and do not receive or transmit signals appropriately.
3. The communication path between the brain and other parts of the body is disrupted, and messages no longer flow past the damaged area.

Have I nerded out too much? If so, I'm sorry. I am a self-proclaimed geek, so it happens. But stick with me. I'm going somewhere with this.

Something cool that I learned through the journey with Todd and not through the science books in high school is when your spinal cord suffers an injury and nerves are severed, your body can rewire itself. Apparently, every nerve has backup nerves. And if the spinal cord injury is not completely severed, your body can rewire itself to have those backup nerves kick in and help what was lost.

Cool stuff, right? When areas of our body fail, they can be rewired to overcome this!

The key to healing mental paralysis is similar to this process. When our mind fails us, God can rewire our brains to overcome this!

Take, for example, Ben. His body went through the process of healing. He had a healthy heart to work hard. His brain had the right mindset to send signals to move. And the communication channel in his spinal cord started healing through "rewiring" to help him figure out how to move again.

But not only did the connections within Ben's body start healing, Ben was mentally healing as well. And this is because his connection with God was in full force. This connection with God gave him incredible hope and strength and will. It helped him mentally drown out the negative signals trying to keep him from working as hard as possible to overcome his paralysis. And he had a connection with God throughout his journey. Because of this, his mind was in the right place to focus on healing and moving again.

When it comes to our mental paralysis, we need to have the right mindset rooted in God. The image below draws the parallel of healing from physical and mental paralysis.

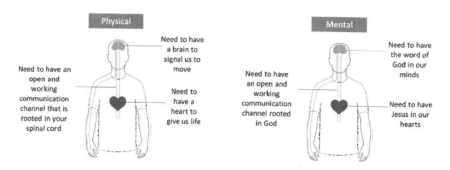

Let's talk about physical paralysis and mental paralysis and the parallels between the two.

HEART — "Our Life Center"

To heal from physical paralysis, we first need our heart to be open and working to be able to recover. Without this, we ain't movin', folks. We dead.

In the case of mental paralysis, we need to have an open and working relationship with God. This relationship with him gives us the will and energy to heal. If we find ourselves in a state of paralysis, there is only one answer. We need a defibrillator. And that defibrillator is Jesus. We need more Jesus in our hearts.

So, what does it mean to have Jesus in our hearts?

Well, first, it means that we have to begin looking at the heart as more than just a physical part of our body. The heart is the center of our emotional lives. It's not just an organ, it's the heart of what we feel, what we believe, and what we are passionate about. And when we ask Jesus to come into our hearts, guess who we are putting in command of that heart center?

That's right, Jesus.

Before choosing to let Jesus be in command, we tend to take up space in the captain's seat. We shape how we feel. We choose what to believe. We determine what we are passionate about. And given our sinful nature, that life center can start to look ugly. We fall victim to worldly ways and Satan's lies. The heart becomes consumed with not just good but evil beliefs, feelings, and passions. Perhaps it's safe to say that the ship regularly gets steered in the wrong direction.

The Bible is full of hearts that were steered in the wrong direction and hearts that paralyzed people from spiritually progressing and overcoming in their lives.

When Paul wrote to the Romans about God's judgment of sin, he wrote specifically about the hardness and stubbornness of the heart.

But because of your hardness and impenitent heart,
you are storing up treasures of wrath against yourself
on the day of wrath when the righteous judgment of God
will be revealed.

Romans 2:5

Paul was essentially calling out the Romans for having judgmental hearts against those who sin when they, in fact, were sinners themselves.

·en do you find yourself doing this? Casting stones when you, in a glass house?

This verse personally makes me think about gossip. Man, do we women love some juicy gossip. For some reason, women tend to gravitate to the side of our hearts that is hard and impenitent, finding platforms behind closed doors to call out other women for their sinful ways. Our sinful selves stand there in judgment of other women's sins, ruthlessly calling attention to the sinful ways of those who would otherwise have no idea. Real nice, huh? And let's not forget to mention that the entire act of gossiping is a sin in itself.

What a yucky, yucky hard heart we can have when we are steering the ship, right? It's just gross.

Hard hearts can come in all sorts of shapes and sizes. They are plentiful in our world today. But when Jesus is in our hearts, it starts to shape it differently. It softens it. And when hearts are softened, so are our feelings and emotions.

Another example of how our hearts can paralyze us was in the Old Testament when the Lord spoke about the rebellious hearts of the Jews.

But my people have stubborn and rebellious hearts.
They have turned away and abandoned me.

Jeremiah 5:23

This verse demonstrates that even God's people are innately rebellious and will turn from God and sin. We are stubborn. We are rebellious. And I have to believe that God sometimes feels that we just leave him in the dust.

I'm sure that you can relate. For anyone who has a teenager, you know exactly what I'm talking about when I talk about a rebellious heart. Man, can teenagers be stubborn. And rebellious.

I've got a friend who's dealing with her teenager who has been smoking pot, stealing, and causing all sorts of havoc. Seriously, what a parenting nightmare, right? This child that mom loves so dearly is rebelling, and no matter what she does, her son can't get his life in control. This can make a mom lose her mind, right?

Well, imagine how God feels with us. We are no different, people. In his eyes, we are equally stubborn and rebellious in our lives. He's trying so desperately to get us walking on the right path with him, and we are rebelling and living in our paralyzed ways.

What a parenting nightmare for God.

How about you? Are there areas in your life where you have a rebellious heart? In what ways do you think you could be a parenting nightmare for God right now?

Rebellious hearts need rehabilitation. They are prime pickings for Satan to infiltrate. The best way to avoid being Satan's prey? *Pray!*

And let's not forget about the role that broken hearts play in being paralyzed in life. David wrote about this:

> *The Lord is close to the brokenhearted; he rescues those*
> *whose spirits are crushed.*
>
> ### Psalm 34:18

When David wrote this, he wasn't just writing this about someone else's experience with a broken heart. He was speaking about his own. If there was anyone in the Bible whose broken heart was on full display, it was David.

David spent years fleeing from people who wanted to kill him. These people happened to be people that he loved and cared for.

David's broken heart led him to live a good part of his life paralyzed by despair and fear. You can read all about it in Psalms.

Like David, there are so many people who are paralyzed with broken hearts. They cannot overcome the trials they have endured, the pain they have suffered, and the longing for things lost.

People who have broken hearts are often referred to as being "crushed in spirit." To be crushed in spirit demonstrates the personal affliction that is taking place within that heart. Is being crushed in spirit even repairable?

It is. Because the spirit that is crushed is our own. It is not the Holy Spirit inside of us. The Holy Spirit cannot be crushed; it is our best lifeline. The Holy Spirit can heal our broken hearts.

In fact, David went on to write in Psalms,

Create in me a clean heart, O God.
Renew a loyal spirit within me.

Psalm 51:10

David made this plea to God after he had taken advantage of another man's wife. Yes, David was an adulterer. But wait, it gets better. David also was a murderer. He killed the husband of the woman he was taking advantage of. David was about as bad of a sinner as one could get.

But David also had a repentant heart for God. He was brokenhearted that he had sinned against God. He knew that he was wrong and saw that God was the cure. He saw that his heart could be restored and renewed, so David stated that confession to God.

And then God responded. God honored David's repentance and restored his heart.

This list could go on about all types of hearts. The Bible talks about troubled hearts, vulnerable hearts, hypocritical hearts, defiled hearts, and more. You name the negative emotion or feeling, and there is a heart for it in the Bible.

The heart that God wants for us all is a transformed heart. One that has been changed by the life and death of Jesus Christ. One that has the Holy Spirit both leasing and managing the space.

Then Christ will make his home in your hearts as you trust
in him. Your roots will grow down into God's love and
keep you strong.

Ephesians 3:17

A transformed heart is the game changer to overcoming the areas in our lives where we are paralyzed. Without Jesus Christ, a burdensome heart is all that will remain. The evil beliefs and thoughts will stay captive.

When we ask Jesus to come into our hearts, it changes how we think, affects our emotions, and impacts our choices. It takes evil beliefs and thoughts, spits them out, and replaces them with love.

One of the areas that God has made a transformation in my heart is with my pride. I do a lot of speaking through my ministry. It's probably my favorite part of my godly mission. But in the early days of my speaking, I found myself more concerned about what people thought of me than what they thought of God.

My mission to speak and write on behalf of God had become too self-centered. I was overly concerned about what people would think of me. Fixated on people liking me. Obsessed with delivering perfection.

I remember the event when this prideful heart became apparent to me. I left it feeling defeated. I obsessed over anything and everything that I said. I reviewed people's faces and expressions in my mind, searching for some acceptance. Me. Me. Me.

God didn't provide the affirmation that I was looking for. He didn't want to. Because it wasn't supposed to be about me. It was supposed to be about him and transforming the hearts of the people in the room.

God showed me that he deserves and needs to be number one. He doesn't appreciate self-righteous pride. When we become consumed with ourselves and all that we have, we are putting ourselves above him. We are taking credit for what God has done.

When I recognized this, it was game-changing for me. Instead of obsessing over people's perceptions of me before an event, I started praying for people to see God shine through me. I put it all in his hands. And when my events were done, instead of replaying every detail in my head, I praised God for what he had done and prayed for Satan's prideful thoughts to stay away.

This was a huge heart transformation for me. And hopefully, it is serving God's purpose of transforming other hearts as well.

What about you? What heart transformation do you think God wants to perform in your life?

The best way to transform a heart is to let God infiltrate it. There are many ways to wade into this, so it's best to start by asking God how *he* wants you to invite him in. Perhaps he wants you to spend every day in prayer. Or maybe he wants to direct you to friends, pastors, devotionals, Bible verses, women's studies, church, and more. Listen to what God is placing in your heart and follow through with it.

As the Holy Spirit fills you, it won't leave space in your heart for the things that are breaking it.

MIND — "Our Signal Center"

There's an essential piece of Scripture that I want to talk about. And that is that our minds and hearts are connected.

In Matthew 9:4, when Jesus was getting ready to heal the paralyzed man in Capernaum and the religious leaders had thoughts of blasphemy stirring within, Jesus said to them,

> *"Why are you thinking evil things in your hearts?"*
>
> **Matthew 9:4 CSB**

"*Thinking* evil things in your *hearts*." Have you ever thought about your heart thinking? I personally have not. I've thought about a heart feeling but not thinking.

This verse shows that our minds and hearts are connected when it comes to thinking. They are simply not stand-alone entities. The two work hand in hand. Think about how our minds impact our physical movement. Our brain sends and receives signals on how we should physically react.

When you take this same concept, it also describes how our minds work when we mentally react, by sending and receiving signals.

When there is spiritual dehydration in our minds, it makes us more susceptible to sin and believing Satan's lies. Satan fills the empty space with negative signals in our brains, such as:

- He will lead someone with social anxieties to believe that they will be rejected if they try to talk to someone.
- He will trick someone who wants to pursue a different career path into believing that they are not qualified.
- He will plant seeds with someone who has been hurt by a relationship to believe that they cannot trust anyone ever again.

This is just a small sample in a huge universe of Satan's lies. He wants to fill our brains with these lies so we remain paralyzed. He loves us there. That evil dude loves your bondage. It's a feature film for him. He's hanging out in there eating popcorn watching your train wreck take place.

To reduce the brain space that Satan fills up, we need to fill it with the ammo of God. That is the word of God. It is the greatest weapon that God has given us.

In fact, think back to the healing of the paralyzed servant. When the Roman officer was afraid of Jesus entering his home to heal his servant, he said to Jesus,

"Just say the word from where you are, and my servant will be healed."

Matthew 8:8

Jesus then commended the officer on his incredible faith and said to him, "Go back home. Because you believed, it has happened."

Jesus revealed through this miracle that he can heal through *his words.* He didn't have to be physically present with the young servant. He didn't have to place his hands on him. He only had to use his words to heal.

If Jesus' words can heal the paralyzed servant, they can heal you. Jesus used this miracle to demonstrate the power his words can have in our lives to heal whatever it is that is paralyzing us. And it just so happens that we have all his words right at our fingertips—in the word of God.

The word of God is the answer to spiritually hydrating our brains. When we rehabilitate our minds with the Bible, we drown out the lies in our brains and fill them with the truth.

> *It is the same with my word. I send it out, and it always*
> *produces fruit. It will accomplish all I want it to, and it*
> *will prosper everywhere I send it.*
>
> ### Isaiah 55:11

The word of God is full of truth signals. We will talk more about signals in the next chapter. Still, it's important to remember that our minds receive signals every second of every day that influence the decisions we make every second of every day. If we aren't receiving truth signals by being present in the word of God, then we are going to continue to deal with the repercussions of spiritual dehydration and the paralysis it brings.

ROOTS — "Our Communication Center"

It's one thing to be receiving signals from God; it's a whole other thing to be applying his word to our lives. Rick Warren, the founder of Saddleback Church, said it best when asked what the best translation of the Bible was. He said, "when you translate it into your life."

I love this quote so much. It's a mic drop.

If we are just receiving God's word signals but aren't translating them into our lives, his words just become words on paper. Your knowledge of those words, your memorization of those words, your reading of those words loses all the power if you aren't translating them into your life.

That means that in order to translate them into our lives, we have to process his words into our life and obey.

Jesus replied, "Anyone who loves me will obey my
teaching. My Father will love them, and we will come to
them and make our home with them."

John 14:23 NIV

When we are called to obey God's teaching as a Christian, we are essentially being called to take a considerable risk. That's what faith is really about, right? It's blindly following a path that God is leading us down.

When we take that risk, have blind faith, and follow God down a path in which we are not in control, that is what we call obedience. To obey God's teachings, we are essentially being asked to take God's word for it and do as he says.

For us to be successful in doing that, we need an open and working connection with God. Our connection with God is the central nervous system of our lives. Without this, nothing moves, nothing works, nothing changes.

I like to use the analogy of the spine. You can't just have a spine and expect to move; you need an open and working communication channel within your spine to be able to move. In other words, the spine alone does nothing, the communication channel flowing through your spinal cord is where the movement happens.

The same goes with the Bible. You can't just stare at the spine of a Bible and be transformed. The Bible has to be open and working for us to connect with it and translate it into our lives. The communication within it is where the movement happens. We have to have an open and working connection with him.

So, what does that communication channel look like for us? It comes in two forms.

- The word of God is God's communication channel *to us.*
- And prayer is our communication *with him.*

To have open and working communication with God, we have to be using these two channels.

I've heard a lot of people say they can't "hear" God. In fact, I used to be one of those people. But when people say this, they mean they are not hearing God's voice during prayer. And that may, in fact, be the case. The truth, however, is that anyone, anywhere, anytime can hear God's voice through reading the Bible. The word of God is God's voice. It is him communicating to us. Right there in black and white. God's words are right at our fingertips, day and night.

When we want to open up a communication channel *with* God, as in two-way communication, that is when prayer comes into play. The Bible talks *a lot* about prayer! There are references to who, what, where, when, why, and how throughout the Bible. These are a few of the key takeaways from Scripture:

WHO: Prayer is for *all believers!* John (9:31)

WHAT: Prayer is for *everything!* (Phil. 4:6–7)

WHERE: Prayer can be done a*nywhere!* (Jonah 2:1)

WHEN: Prayer should be done *all the time!* (1Thes. 5:16–18)

WHY: Prayers are answered by God! (Mat. 21:22)

HOW: Prayer should be accompanied with *belief and no doubt!* (Mark 11:22)

Prayer is essential to living a better, healthier life. Having this communication channel with God open and working is such an important part of our recovery process and our walk with God.

This leads me to a personal story. Any other husband would possibly be terribly upset at this story being shared. But Todd is cool. So, I'll share anyway.

On the third day of the accident, when Todd was still paralyzed, he shared with the doctor that he felt like he needed to go to the bathroom. As in number two. It had not happened since the accident, and we did not really understand the gravity of that until we saw the doctor's reaction.

His rehabilitation doctor, who was an extremely stone-cold serious woman, lit up like a Lite Brite. Smiling from ear to ear, she erupted, "This is great news!"

As you can imagine, Todd and I were very confused.

"Todd's butt is the last spot on the spinal cord. This means the super communication highway is open for business!" the doctor explained.

Little did we know that Todd's urge to go would be the indicator that his spinal cord injury was incomplete. This meant that the communication channel in his spinal cord was still open and working.

This changed everything.

Todd, indeed, had a chance to heal. God had been right all along.

I share this story with you because this story translates into your life too. If you have a relationship with God, your super communication highway to him is open for business! This communication channel is the pathway to healing and helping us mentally move from the things that are paralyzing you in your life. When it's open for business, it means he's ready to get you moving!

I can promise you when you realize this and open up that communication channel, I imagine God reacts like Todd's doc reacted. He's elated! He's smiling! He's screaming, "This is great news!"

Hope changes. Attitude changes. Mission changes.

For you are God, O Sovereign Lord. Your words are true,
and you have promised these good things to your servant.

2 Samuel 7:28

Revealing Questions

When each of these areas in our life—the heart, mind, and rooted connection with God—is restored from being broken, we are able to move from those things that are paralyzing us.

Take some time to reflect on each of these areas in your life right now.

1. Your Heart — "Your Life Center"

Is your heart open or blocked? Is it full of positive emotions or negative? Would you say that your heart has been transformed? How is your heart commanding you?

2. Your Mind — "Your Signal Center"

What is currently saturating your brain right now? Are you experiencing paralyzing thoughts? Is it filled with the truth of God? Would you say that your mind has been transformed? What signals is your mind sending you?

3. Your Roots — "Your Communication Center"

What communication are you rooted in regularly? Is it communication with God? Are you filling yourself with positive daily communication? Would you say that your communication roots have been transformed? How are you acting on the communication you are receiving from God?

Level the Devil

So humble yourselves before God. Resist the devil,
and he will flee from you.

James 4:7

Most often, when people are paralyzed, they think it's something that they cannot change. The power of what's controlling them is too difficult to break. In many cases, the power it has on them is so great that they stop trying to change it altogether and just come to accept that it is the way their life is going to be. Even some, perhaps, consider themselves one of the unlucky ones.

Well, these thoughts are a bunch of malarkey.

There have been far too many people who can testify that they beat significant odds to overcome the impossible for anyone to believe those statements are true. I'm sure you know or are aware of some pretty incredible stories of people defeating things that trapped them for many years.

This "power" that we believe is paralyzing us isn't power at all. It's just lies. Lies sent by the evil one himself. Satan.

The truth is Satan has no power over us at all. He can only influence our thoughts. He cannot physically force you to do or not to do something. He can't . . .

- restrain you from leaving a bad situation.
- hold your hands back from typing up your resume.
- lift a fork of third helpings to your face.
- push you down so you stay lying in bed all day.
- make your mouth move to form the vial things coming out of it.

Nope. He does not have this power.

What he does instead is influence our thoughts so we *choose* to continue living in our paralysis. He is not exerting physical power over us to make us live in our paralysis. He is lying, deceiving, and placing a whole lot of fear in our thoughts so we *choose* to stay stuck.

Let's face it, Satan is just a big ol' meanie. And while it would be nice to just flick him right off our shoulders, the fact is that we can't. So, we need to figure out how to thwart off his attacks when they are happening.

It all starts with the communication signals we are processing in our lives.

God Signals

Let's recap how the brain works. The brain receives and transmits signals to the rest of our body to react. While our brains are brilliant and powerful machines that ultimately dictate our lives, they are susceptible to infiltration. Satan sees this as his doorway into our world.

When we are paralyzed, it means that the big ol' meanie is intercepting our signals with lies, and we are responding accordingly. For example, Satan often makes us think

- overcoming our paralysis will cause a danger that doesn't even exist.
- we are not worthy of love and need to live a life without it.
- we are justified in holding on to our anger.
- that God can't change our circumstances.

These are bogus lies! Satan is a brain invader! He's a mind intruder! We have the *choice* to not let him in!

Let's put this in perspective and get physical again here for a minute. Our lives are made up of responding to signals every second of every day. The brain responds to signals in two ways:

- Choice: where we cognitively make a decision to do something, and then our brain sends a signal to do it (like stopping at a stoplight).

- Automatic: where the brain is making that decision and sending a signal to do it without making a choice (like breathing or blinking).

Now let's look at how this applies to your life. Our circumstances are influenced by one of two things:

- the decisions we make (choices)
- the situations we are in (automatically)

The signals we get that help us make every decision in your lives are either:

- influenced by God (where all the good exists)
- influenced by the outside world (where Satan lurks)

We have little control over our automatic circumstances. We don't get to choose them. But we do get to choose how we deal with them. It's in our *choices* that we become susceptible to the outside world. This allows Satan to creep in, and then those lies linger too long. These signals influence us every day, and in doing so, they interrupt the signals that make us mentally move. We then become *paralyzed.*

Satan's mission is to stop us from living the life that God intends for us. He will give us every reason to be complacent and use our struggles against us. He will make us fearful to move. He will do anything with his lies to paralyze us from God's will for our lives. For instance, Satan will

- encourage an abused woman to feel like it's her fault.
- convince an alcoholic that just one more drink won't hurt anyone.
- deceive a woman to believe she can never follow her dreams.
- tell a skinny teenage girl that she is fat and should not eat.
- scare a codependent from reinforcing boundaries for fear of reaction.

There are all types of paralysis on all kinds of levels. We all have our own paralysis, and various influences from Satan impacting our recovery.

This paralysis, caused by the evil space invader in our minds, results from the irrational thoughts he fills us with. We may think,

- "What's the point?"
- "There's no hope."
- "I'm not good enough."
- "I have no control of this."
- "I have control of this!"

These thoughts are complete lies among a list of many. Brought to you by the world's most incredible liar, liar, pants on fire.

But Satan's lies do not have the power that God's power has. With God's power, we can push aside Satan's hold on us and walk down the path that God has created for us.

What we need to recognize is that through God, our choices can change. If we have God in our lives, then we can more clearly hear *his* signals. And then subsequently, we can dismiss those irrational thoughts.

God's signals can single-handedly drown out Satan's. He's that good and that powerful.

When we pursue the signals God is giving us and we make our choices based on that, guess what? Our outcomes change! And when our outcomes change, what happens? We have the opportunity to move again!

As I'm writing this, Satan is literally attacking me. What a total jerk. I guess he doesn't want you clued in to this truth at all. Right now, he's telling me,

- "You're writing is stupid."
- "You are never going to get this book done."
- "You are not qualified to write any of this."
- "Wouldn't you rather be drinking wine right now?"

I pause now to pray.

And now I say out loud, "In the name of Jesus, evil influences be gone!"

Ugh, seriously, I'm so sick of his crap! He's been trying to stop this book for too long—five years!

There is no stopping Satan and his antics. But we can thwart his efforts by recognizing the three ways that Satan has mastered invading our brains: squirrels, attacks, and dirty work.

Satan's Squirrels

My husband kindly refers to my attention issue as squirrel chasing. He is well aware of my issues and softly says the word "squirrel" when I veer off course—such a kind man with such a kind correction.

But my kind husband is not the only one aware of my problem. The big ol' meanie is too. Satan has been doing everything he can to keep me from getting to the finish line of this book. I've been chasing more squirrels than my English Springer Spaniel. And my dog is a complete savage.

There have been times that I've been so ashamed of the squirrel chasing I've done that I sat on my couch with a blanket over my head to hide my shame of chasing squirrels from God. For real. As if this blanket would block God's view of it! And as if he wasn't on my side of this ordeal. I mean, c'mon. God sent me on this mission, and he certainly has had my back.

But I would be lying to you if I told you that this process has been easy. I cannot even begin to count the squirrels Satan has thrown at me in the last four years. But here's a few of them.

Satan told me to sell our house. Mr. Lyin' Eyes told me that in order to leave my past behind, I needed a fresh, new start. And that I needed a new home to do so. So, I spent months getting ready to sell our house, searching for a new place, putting it on the market, showing it, blah, blah, blah. I got to the point of even accepting an offer.

Then, I finally started listening to what God had been stirring in my heart. I didn't need to leave my house to leave my past behind. I just needed to give it to God. When I finally did that, my walls looked different. It was full of eighteen years of memories with my children. Memories that had been hidden away behind hard times were suddenly recaptured. It was as if a fog had lifted and the sun was shining bright. I saw my home in a completely different light.

Fortunately, an opportunity opened for us to back out of selling our house. Crisis averted. We were able to stay.

But all of this could have been avoided if I wouldn't have chased this squirrel. If I wouldn't have believed the lies that Satan was sending my way. If I would have leaned into God sooner.

Satan also tempted me with lots of shiny objects. Searching for a lake house, putting in a pool, going on vacations, and on and on and on. All things we couldn't afford. If only I had this, then I would be happy. If only I had that, then I would have more peace to write this book. If only. If only. If only.

"If only" squirrels are some of the biggest distractions that he will use against us. These are those "worldly way" signals he uses to lure us—all sexy and such.

The Bible addresses how we should handle all types of squirrel temptations. Paul wrote:

> *No temptation has overtaken you that is not common*
> *to man. God is faithful, and he will not let you be tempted*
> *beyond your ability, but with the temptation he will*
> *also provide the way of escape, that you may be able*
> *to endure it.*

1 Corinthians 10:13 ESV

You see, squirrel chasing is something we all experience. Squirrel chasing in and of itself is really just giving into some level of temptation. It might be big temptations or small temptations that lead us off course of living the life that God intends for us.

Chasing squirrels is so easy to do. When life gets hard, gets challenging, gets ready for a significant change, Satan will dangle super sexy squirrels in front of you to veer you off course. He doesn't want you to find the rescue. He wants you to think there is an easier way out. He wants to distract you from changing your life. He wants anything but the life that God has intended for you.

Satan's Attacks

No doubt squirrel chasing has had its impact on *our* lives. And in this ministry. But God has also used them.

The one thing that I never expected to happen as I embarked on this ministry was the constant battles I was going to face. I was undoubtedly overwhelmed and nervous about it all, but I didn't expect the attacks.

Satan, the big bully, has been pulling punches left and right. He's been Mike Tyson ... I've been little ol' me, getting pummeled. Gashes-above-my-brow, black-around-my-eye, gauze-stuck-in-my-nose pummeled. Throughout this journey, I've had moments when I've been ready to tap out.

He's tried it all.

At one point in time, I was preparing for my very first large workshop. I was expecting close to one hundred ladies in the room, and I was responsible for about five hours of their time that day.

As with any squirrel chaser, I found myself running out of time and trying to squeeze in preparations at the last possible minute to prepare for the event. A few days before the event, I had an hour between work meetings in a town nearby. I decided to go to a nearby grocery store with a Starbucks and a restaurant and get on my computer.

As I was standing in the line at the Starbucks, the PA system turned on, and out came the devil's voice. At least what I thought the devil's voice sounded like. Not lyin'. This low, screeching, incoherent, slow, creepy voice. It sent chills down my spine.

I sat there motionless for a moment to see if anyone else was hearing what I was hearing. No one moved. I got more creeped out. Finally, I turned to the person next in line and said, "That is really creepy." They replied, "I totally agree." Phew. I was not losing it.

This voice proceeded to go on for about the next ten minutes. It was disturbing enough that it drove people out of the store. While I realized that what was really going on was likely an issue with the PA system, deep down inside, I think Satan was using this situation to creep me out enough to not get that fifty minutes of content created. He wanted to scare me away.

He had a history of that, after all. He had become a master in sinking me with irrational thoughts. And when I turned my computer on to find my laptop imploding with the black screen of death, he almost had me drowning. All of that work lost. Crisis!

But then my God signals interceded, and I was able to sink Satan's thoughts rather than letting them sink me. Sure enough, the computer rebooted fine, and all was not lost.

In reality, Satan's failed attempt to attack me just gave me more material. I went into that restaurant, and I wrote. I wrote about my squirrel chasing. I used it in my presentation. In fact, squirrel chasing was my opener.

Satan's attacks are no good until we recognize them and put them to rest. When we do that, God will use it for good.

Being able to discern what is an attack from Satan is the hard part. Man, is that evil dude a trickster. He will do anything and everything in his power to mess with us. The master of manipulation.

When my anxiety was at its height kicking my butt, I had a confidant share with me a way to identify an attack from Satan. It's a pretty quick and easy test that I use day in and day out.

When you try to overcome your paralysis and a thought comes to your mind that has you worried, fearful, angry, upset, or any other negative feeling, ask yourself these two questions.

1. Is this thought based on TRUTH?

In other words, can the thought be scripturally supported? Is there anything in the Bible that contradicts this thought? Or you can use the good ol' litmus test of WWJD. (What would Jesus do.)

2. Is this thought based on FACT?

Is it something factual that can support your thought? Are you witnessing actual danger or imagining danger? Is it in your sight or in your imagination?

If you cannot say yes to either of those questions, you can dismiss it as a lie from Satan. He's trying to attack you.

Satan even tried tricking Jesus! When Jesus was led by the Spirit into the wilderness to fast for forty days and forty nights, the big ol' meanie came in for the attack. He tried to get Jesus to do the opposite of what God had commanded him to do on three separate occasions.

> *During that time the devil came and said to him, "If you are the Son of God, tell these stones to become loaves of bread." But Jesus told him, "No! The Scriptures say, 'People do not live by bread alone, but by every word that comes from the mouth of God.'"*
>
> ### Matthew 4:3–4

Satan tried to attack Jesus by catching him when he was famished and weak. He will do the same to us, trying to attack us in our weakness.

But look what Jesus used as a weapon against that attack. He used *truth*. He used Scripture to fight back and defeat Satan. Look at the words in the Scripture that he used. "People do not live by bread alone, but by *every word that comes from the mouth of God*" (Matthew 4:4).

This is so, so powerful. Jesus is teaching us in this very moment how to resist Satan by using the word of God.

Truth is our greatest weapon. When we are armed with it, even in our weakness, Satan can be stopped. It is our armor. It is our shield. It is our sword. Use all of it to destroy Satan's attacks.

Satan's Dirty Work

As we become more and more resilient in resisting Satan's attacks in our day-to-day lives, it requires him to use even more deceitful tactics. Satan is, after all, masterful at distracting and attacking our brains. It's the center of his wicked scheme. Satan is not only the master of attacking us in our every day, he is also the master of not ever letting our pasts and the pasts of others go.

Satan preys upon the things in our pasts that paralyze us or that paralyze others. They are prime picking for him. He sees the pain still residing. He sees the guilt still lurking. And he sees the wounds still bleeding.

He tricks us into believing that the things that paralyze us or others should be unearthed forever and ever. He's like a skid loader: everyday, digging up the dirt in our lives and the dirt in others. Satan is the master at dirty work.

The slang use for the word "dirt" is used regularly as reference to negative information about someone. We toss dirt around as we gossip about others. And people toss it around as they gossip about us.

What many people don't know is that the origin for the word dirt was actually "poop." Yep. Pig poop, as a matter of fact. So, if we own it, we can stake claim to playing a part in spreading poop for Satan. He's a manure mover. And so are we.

Why do we do this? Why do we take these painful wounds in peoples' lives and treat them like worthless, dirty smut? And, in the same light, why do we view the sins of our owns pasts that are paralyzing us in the same negative light?

> *Therefore, if anyone is in Christ, he is a new creation. The old has passed away; behold, the new has come.*
>
> ### *2 Corinthians 5:17 ESV*

We need to recognize that we do not need to keep unburying our sins when we have asked God for forgiveness. When our past sins died on the cross with Jesus, they were intended to remain dead. When we choose, instead, to dig them up, we are resurrecting something that should never be resurrected.

We are given new lives through Christ.

Live. That. Life.

Keep that sin buried. Forever.

But the same goes for your neighbor, friend, family, co-worker, or your waitress. They too deserve the chance to bury their sin with Christ. And how can they do that when you are unearthing it for the whole world to hear?

I know I already harped on this when I talked about hardened hearts. And girls, I know this one is super tough. Women are gossipers. I don't know why, but we are. I can tell you that even in my church and among my closest Christian friends, we struggle with this.

It is absolutely one of the hardest things for me to keep in check. But we have to stop. Girls, we have to. Not only is it the right thing to do, but we are also called to do it. We are held to an even higher standard here. Because regardless of whether they know Christ, you do. And you are called by him to not dig up dirt on other people.

Gossip is addressed in the Bible for these significant reasons.

- Gossip divides people.
- Gossip is toxic.
- Gossip is a lack of self-control.
- Gossip is judging.

Why do we feel such satisfaction in gossiping? Is it because it makes us feel better to point out someone else's paralysis, so we don't have to focus on our own? Does it make us feel better about our own poorly run lives if we focus on how crappy someone else's is?

I recall visiting with a friend once when she shared the story about a couple who was going through a divorce. There was a lot of drama going on. You know, scandalous. It was, like so many of these, a juicy story. What gossipers crave.

I allowed the gossip to continue, so I also bear responsibility and shame here. But I was uncomfortable with it. And that conversation changed my view on gossip forever.

What bothered me so much about that conversation was the smile on her face. The laughter. The enjoyment she had when sharing about someone else's strife. It was like the yummiest dessert she had ever eaten, and she was just lapping it up.

I've never looked at that friend the same. I've never trusted her again. I've imagined the stones that she's thrown at my house. This gossip separated us.

A troublemaker plants seed of strife;
gossip separates the best of friends.

Proverbs 16:28

We have to do better, girls. Gossip is Satan's weapon. When you are doing it, you are bearing his sword. Not God's. Just think about that for a minute.

Satan will never stop trying to do his dirty work through you.

I believe that it is no accident that Jesus was born to us amid dirt and poop. The Son of God came to us in a place that represented our very lives.

But he didn't continue living in it.

Out of it came the most perfect, clean, sinless man to have ever walked this earth. And while we will never, ever live to be the perfect man that he was, by following him, obeying him, and emulating him, we get to leave the dirt behind too.

Revealing Questions

When Satan infiltrates our signals through squirrels, attacks, and dirty work, it can paralyze us and take us off course of living the lives that God intends for us.

Take some time to reflect on how Satan might be being a space-invader in your mind right now and what you can do to overcome it.

1. Squirrels

When it comes to the areas that you are paralyzed, what distractions are being dangled in front of you to keep you from overcoming? What worldly things are you being tempted with that feel like the perfect fix? How can you turn to God to help you navigate these temptations? What would be the upside to eliminating these things from your life?

2. Attacks

How is Satan currently attacking you? What lies do you uncover when you determine that your thoughts are not based on truth or fact? What scriptural warfare could you memorize to help arm you against these attacks?

3. Dirty Work

Do you find yourself frequently gossiping about other people? When you do, what feelings does that give you? How do you feel when you discover others gossiping about you? Would those feelings align with God's work or with Satan's work? What are some steps you can take to help you navigate these situations in a Godly way?

Paralysis Analysis

Paul's final advice:
Examine yourselves, to see where you are in faith.
Test yourselves. Or do you not realize this about
yourselves, that Jesus Christ is in you?—
unless indeed you fail to meet the test!

2 Corinthians 13:5 ESV

So, I was sitting in church one day listening to our phenomenal pastor. He just has a way with connecting to his people. He's personable, relatable, and real. You know the type.

Everything in service that day spoke to me.

The worship. The message. And the mistake.

Yes, the mistake.

Let me explain. Our pastor is tremendously gifted. Every Sunday, he delivers these amazing messages that just hit ya. As if they were written specifically for you. He has a knack for pointing us closer to God every Sunday.

This particular Sunday was no different. His message was focused on the guardrails God has put in our lives to direct us and protect us. It resonated so deeply with me. I needed guardrails in my life. The message completely captivated me.

And then there it was.

A tipo.

I mean a typo.

There it was in the midst of the projected screen, a simple "i" missing from a single word. This typo was so small it was practically hidden. But I saw it. I have to imagine that others saw it too.

Suddenly, I couldn't see past it. Despite my pastor's valiant and powerful delivery of the word of God, my brain couldn't focus on his message anymore. Instead, I was thinking,

Do you think he knows it's there?

Do others see it?

What would his English teacher think?

There my pastor was, doing everything right. Doing what God called him to do. And bam, that best effort was disrupted. Although small, it managed to be, at least for me, a distraction on God's purpose for the morning.

It made me think about how this is what happens in our lives too. We do our absolute best to do our very best. But despite that, we still have imperfections that may seem obvious to others, but that we don't even realize we have. And as small as it may seem, these little things in our lives that we are too blind to see can, in some ways, paralyze our godly purpose.

When we think we are a shining light, changing lives, there are people surrounding us thinking,

- Do you think she knows about this imperfection?
- Do others see it too?
- How has she not done anything about it?
- What must people think of her?

Fortunately, in the story of my pastor, the distraction was short. There was no harm done. No need for correction. Grace was given.

But when it comes to our life imperfections, those surrounding us don't always handle it in the same way. Oftentimes, it's too hard for them to move past it or give grace. And in some cases, when we really need them to shine light on it to help us get corrected, they run.

While there is a Christian duty to help steer people away from the things that are paralyzing them, we can't put the onus on others to help us make the correction in our lives. We need to take some ownership to try to see the things that are paralyzing us that, maybe, we just can't see.

We need to take the time to proofread our lives.

Let's face it. When we are pounding away, doing all we can to meet all our life expectations, we don't spend a whole lot of time looking at the life we live.

We aren't proofreading our lives to find our sins and imperfections and working on correcting them. We can be very unaware of our life typos. All the while, those staring at our life stories straight in the face every day are noticing. And if it stands out more than the efforts you are making to do good things in the world and for God, then it's time to make a change.

It's time to proofread our lives. To eliminate those typos that distract the lives of those we love and paralyze us from living the life that God intends for us. It's time to do some paralysis analysis.

Search me, God, and know my heart;
test me and know my anxious thoughts.

Psalm 139:23

Paralysis Analysis

Since you started reading this book, I would imagine that you have had a few ideas bouncing around in your head of things that are paralyzing you. If so, great start. On the contrary, some of you may not have had anything come to mind. If so, it's okay. I'm going to share in this chapter a couple of processes you can go through to help you identify the areas in your life where you are paralyzed.

This can be a challenging exercise, but I will tell you, it's worth it to see it. It's worth recognizing all the things holding you back and getting the courage to get moving again.

Case in point, when I first put myself through this exercise, I identified that for one-third of my life, I was paralyzed with codependency.

When we are so close to the things that make us stuck, we can be oblivious to the years that are flashing by. Seriously, one third of my life! That's just nuts! Ladies, hear me. We can't give paralysis another minute of our lives. Our lives are ticking away!

I also discovered that for almost one-third of my life, I ignored my dream to pursue the purposeful life that God had for me. Yes, for a third of my life, I had put God on hold. Thank God, he is patient! I had put God in the backseat while I drove around aimlessly, finding streets that looked charming only to discover they were dead-end roads.

And how about this one. I determined I had been paralyzed for one tenth of my life with an unfinished house project. This might not seem like a big deal, but this unfinished business seriously drove me to the brink of insanity! I spent ten percent of my life going nuts!

Think about your life. Are there things in your life that have paralyzed you for too long? Are there things that have been driving you to the brink of insanity?

The truth is that the things that paralyze us can be big or small. They come in all shapes and sizes. Things could be stealing your peace every day. Every. Single. Day.

Shed Some Light

The first assessment I like to encourage people to do is what I call the PORCH assessment. Here's the idea behind it.

There are a lot of things we are each hiding from the outside world. We may appear to others that we have it all together, but in reality, what lies behind that white picket fence is not what it seems to be.

We keep our issues shut tight in our personal space for no one to discover. You could say we are sitting in our homes with our blinds shut tight so that no one can see the darkness that lurks inside. But it's in that darkness where our paralysis exists. It's where we feel stuck. It's suffocating. And it's what is keeping us from progressing in our lives.

To start moving toward progress in your life, you have to start by identifying what paralyzes you. Don't worry. This isn't requiring us to go out in the street and shout our problems to the whole world. We just need to walk out onto our front porch and shine a little light on it to see it.

PORCH represents . . .

Pasts - difficult things we cannot move past

Ourselves - personalities, character, environments (i.e., work, home, church, social, etc.)

Relationships - unhealthy or unresolved

Choices - unhealthy habits or choices

Health - mental or physical health decisions

As you think about the PORCH categories, begin to ask yourself these questions.

- What makes me feel helpless?
- What makes me feel stuck?
- What makes me feel fearful?
- What makes me feel incomplete?
- What makes me feel powerless?

Where in your life are you suffering from these symptoms of paralysis? Are there some things that come to mind? There is nothing too big or too small. As I said before, paralysis comes in all sorts of shapes and sizes. There's no limit to what can steal our joy and peace. There's no prescription on what can leave us living in constant fear and living a life that is spinning out of control.

Now ask yourself, how long have you been suffering from this? How much of your life has it been consuming you? Take a moment to pause and calculate this in years. Divide that number by how old you are to arrive at the percentage of your life that you've been struggling with it.

How does that number look to you?

My guess is it might be a real gut punch to see. But rest assured that you are not alone in your battle. Every single person who walks this earth has been paralyzed with something in their lives for too long. There should be no shame, no guilt, no regrets.

Why? Because Jesus washed this all away for us. When he died for us on the cross, he washed this away. He healed us from our paralysis at that moment. When Jesus tells you, "Rise up and walk," he is directing you to move from the paralyzing areas of your life. He is commanding you to let go.

How does it feel to hear that? How does it feel to know that God has let go of that thing that has had you miserable and stuck for too long?

Hopefully, it makes you feel incredible! Hopeful! Unstoppable!

Let me reinforce the importance of this instruction. God is *commanding* you to let go. He is not suggesting. He is not kindly asking. He is not gently prodding. He is your officer, and you are his warrior! He's commanding you, because if you don't do as he says—that is, let go of the things paralyzing you—then you can't be as strong of a warrior as he needs you to be!

But I'm not going to lie to you. Following this command is not easy to do. I've carried my crap for a long time. And I know many of you have too. You might feel that letting go is impossible. You may feel that there is no hope. You may feel that this is out of your control.

You are not alone. I am with you. And I know there are a lot of people just like us.

Take, for instance, my friend Rebecca. I got to know her after she attended one of my workshops, and we kept in touch.

Rebecca had been in an abusive relationship for over twenty years. This was a very broken, unhealthy situation. As bad as it could get.

When I met her, she was in the stage of her paralysis where she knew something needed to change. But it had been impossible for her to leave in the past. She had filed for divorce several different times but never had the courage to follow through with it. She was stuck—the epitome of paralyzed.

Here was this amazing woman with incredible faith who was utterly held captive as a codependent. She was unable to give complete control of her situation to God. She was living a life of constant fear:

- fear of financial stability
- fear of her children hating her

- fear of God not approving
- fear of her husband
- fear of the unknown life beyond it all

Can you imagine the intensity of her situation? And yet, I hear so often people talking about women in abusive situations negatively.

"It's her own fault she didn't leave the guy."

"Why would she stay with him?"

"What the hell's wrong with her?"

Heck, in this situation, the very Christian support she had told her not to discuss her situation anymore because she hadn't left him as they advised.

Hearing this reaction from her support network really concerned me. As if their commands would speed up the faithful process it takes to walk out of that situation. They didn't hold that kind of power. And clearly, it wasn't working for her. For one reason,

Rebecca had to be a *willing participant.*

She had to be willing to go to God and trust him fully and completely to *safely* get her out of that situation. Without her 100% total commitment to that process, it would have ended in failure. Rebecca's faith in God to overcome the impossible was her only avenue to freedom.

And she found that blind faith in him.

And she followed his direction.

And she found freedom.

Rebecca did it. She placed her fears in God's hands. She surrendered her paralysis fully to God. And he led her to freedom.

Just like Rebecca, finding freedom from the things that paralyze us in our lives does not happen overnight. It's a journey that takes constant work.

But the bondage, we can break. Jesus promised this:

So if the Son sets you free, you are truly free.

John 8:36

How do we start taking advantage of this? How do we begin to pursue this freedom that Jesus so desperately desires for us?

We start by cleaning out our garbage.

Cleaning Out the Garbage

Recently I went through the dreaded process of spring cleaning. And I'm not talking about the kind of cleaning that involves Windex and Pledge (or Norwex if you are environmentally conscious). I'm talking about the type of cleaning that involves stuff. Getting rid of lots of stuff. Mostly, it was a bunch of garbage. And piles of it.

We went through our garage, our storage room, our kids' rooms . . . every room. There was so much stuff hiding, we didn't even know how much stuff we had. Piles and piles of stuff were found and eventually thrown upon our stuff pile outside the back door.

By the time we were done, we had enough stuff piled up, it could have housed some small children. In fact, this pile reminded me of the Shel Silverstein poem, "Sarah Cynthia Sylvia Stout Would Not Take the Garbage Out." Sarah's garbage covered all the space on the floor, broke windows, and blocked her front door!

Okay, okay, maybe ours wasn't that bad. But I couldn't believe how much useless, big, painful, gross garbage was in our lives, taking up space. The stuff seemed never ending, and it was exhausting.

We made our trek to the dump with our trailer packed full. There, we got to permanently remove the garbage from our lives. The process of unloading was still painful, disgusting, and arduous. But it was also incredibly satisfying. We were freed from the garbage, and that freedom felt so good.

This is how stuff works in our lives too. Some of our stuff is good, and some of our stuff is garbage. The garbage typically takes up too much space in our lives. Some of that garbage might stink a whole lot. Some of it might be incredibly painful to handle. Some might be very heavy for us to carry. And some of it might be so hidden that we don't know it's even there.

But it is there. And whether we want to or not, we need to recognize the need to clean that garbage out of our lives. Even though we know that the journey to clean it out might be incredibly painful, heavy to carry, and a lot of hard work. And even though it can make us feel sick, we have to go through the process of removing it from our lives to find that freedom.

It may take days, months, or even years to go through our garbage and remove it, but when we do, we can then leave it in the dump. We don't have to lug it back in and let it pile up again. We can leave it at the foot of the cross and trust that God will help us continue to be free of that garbage in our lives.

So, where can you start?

We covered some of this when we discussed the PORCH exercise—analyzing our past, ourselves, relationships, choices, and health and determining what burdens you've been carrying too long. It's a phenomenal exercise to uncover those big, heavy pieces of garbage in our lives.

But what about the rest? What about the more minor things that are taking up too much space in your life? Those things that are creating a heap outside your back door that don't seem worth it to even going through—what about that stuff?

Some stuff requires us to dig even deeper.

Fruit of the Spirit Test

> *But the Holy Spirit produces this kind of fruit in our lives: love, joy, peace, patience, kindness, goodness, faithfulness, gentleness, and self-control. There is no law against these things!*
>
> ### *Galatians 5:22–23*

Perhaps the greatest litmus test we can use when measuring the paralysis in our lives is by comparing the recipe of the Fruit of the Spirit to the recipe we are using for our lives.

Think about it. If you are baking something, and it calls for sugar, but you instead use salt just because you want to or because it's what someone gave you instead, it's going to taste like crap. You won't enjoy the result and neither will anyone that you share it with. Bleh.

In life, we often behave in the same way. We replace the way we should be with the way we want to be, whether it's good for our life or not. Or we accept something from someone the way they want to give it rather than the way they should give it. In both instances, either you or someone else isn't going to enjoy the result. Bleh.

The Fruit of the Spirit is what has been placed in us by the Holy Spirit. Anything and everything that it produces in our lives is good—the result to be enjoyed all around. There is no "bleh" in the world of the Holy Spirit's fruit: love, joy, peace, patience, kindness, goodness, faithfulness, gentleness, and self-control.

In my opinion, there isn't a person in the world that can read those words without having positive thoughts. Who wouldn't desire to have their lives consumed with them? Who wouldn't want to taste that sweetness for the rest of their lives?

So, why not make that the measurement for what also needs to be removed from your lives? Why not identify what's taking the place of that fruit in your life? What is making the sweetness in your life taste like salt instead?

Keep in mind, these don't have to be heavy things. These can be small things that surface in your day that you don't even recognize are ruining it.

Take, for example, my husband. He cannot handle slow left-lane drivers. It makes him completely bonkers. My sweet, gentle, kind, loving husband turns into a shouting, impatient, out-of-control looney. While perhaps a temporary situation, we all know too well how these tiny things can affect the entire mood of the day. The negative result can be lasting. Even aftershocks can follow that minor quake.

What's causing big quakes, and what's causing the little tremors in your life?

To start, ask yourself the questions below. Make sure you don't stop at measuring just the profound. Look at all the ingredients existing in your life. Weigh all the moments of your days.

- What's stealing your joy?
- What makes you feel unloved?
- What ruins your peace?
- What makes you impatient?
- What keeps you from being kind?
- What's driving your bad choices?
- What's tempting you to be unfaithful?
- What's stopping you from being gentle?
- What makes you lose control?

Take some time to escape, pray, and think about each of these. Then come back.

If you have determined that your answers to these questions are not from the fruit, it's time to work on it and let it go. If you have been working on it and can't let it go, you need to recognize that you are paralyzed by it, and it's time to turn to God to help you.

When I answered the questions above, I recognized that my control keeps me from living a life defined by the fruit. When things don't go the way that I try to control, I can become harsh, angry, and sometimes even rageful. In turn, that destroys the peace, love, and joy in my relationships. My control issues can single-handedly destroy the Fruit of the Spirit qualities that I try to carry in my life.

This leads to the ironic question: if I can't control myself, why am I trying to control everyone around me? Self-control is the fruit that I need to be working on the hardest, and when I get that in check, the rest of my fruit won't be as disrupted.

What about you? Which fruit can you give over to God to help it grow? What is keeping you from living a life filled with it?

David's Paralysis

One of the best examples in the Bible of someone analyzing their paralysis, then turning to God for healing was King David. David found himself paralyzed with fear multiple times in his life.

I am losing all hope; I am paralyzed with fear.

Psalm 143:4

If I were to venture a guess, this statement resonates as deeply with you as it does me. Most of us face something in our lives that leaves us feeling hopeless and so paralyzed with fear that we cannot move beyond it.

My list is abundant. I've been paralyzed with fear in pursuing the purpose that God placed in my heart. Paralyzed with fear that someone close to me would take their life. Paralyzed with fear that I might be dying. Paralyzed with fear that my world might fall apart. The list could go on and on.

What about you? What is paralyzing you or has paralyzed you with fear?

As you revisit the things you identified in the prior paralysis analysis exercises, how many of those could you say are attributed to fear?

- Are you fearful of making a change?
- Are you fearful of giving something up?
- Are you fearful of being hurt?
- Are you fearful of missing out?
- Are you fearful of saying goodbye?

Fear comes in all shapes and sizes. There are no predetermined parameters for what it looks like or who it impacts. Even those who feel and appear strong experience fear.

Take, for example, King David. David started out life as just a shepherd boy who was living in his brother's shadows. He wasn't exactly the favorite child. When David was younger, Samuel was sent to anoint one of Jesse's sons as the next king of Israel to replace King Saul. Because David wasn't even on his father's radar, all of the brothers were presented to Samuel except David.

Turns out, none of his brothers were up to snuff, so they sent for David, who was out in the field. And as you can guess, David became the chosen one and was anointed as the next king of Israel.

Eventually, David got so popular as a king and strong warrior that it started making Saul jelly. Apparently, his anointed king was just too awesome for his liking. This is where it starts to go wrong.

Saul went on a mission to have David killed . . . a few different times. I mean, c'mon, David was even Saul's son-in-law! David spent a significant amount of his time fleeing the hatemonger who wanted to kill him, living fearfully in the wilderness and taking residence in caves. Fun times, right?

It wasn't just Saul that led to David's fearful struggles. It was David himself. He was a sinner, and the stuff that he did was naughty enough to have significant consequences.

As it would turn out, one of those consequences was that David's own son, Absalom, also wanted to kill him. Ouch. That's a hard nut to crack.

This sent David fleeing once again, in deep despair and fear. As found in the Psalms, one thing King David documented well was his despair. He was continuously fighting in battles where he was outnumbered. Two men he continually loved tried to kill him. He found himself in more dangerous situations than I could ever imagine.

The despair he felt when fleeing his very own son who was trying to kill him is where we find him in Psalm 143.

Paralyzed with fear.

But there was a difference-maker for David.

He had a profound love for God. Throughout his life, he continuously communicated with God: asking for his guidance, crying out to him, speaking to him. David spent his whole life in conversation with God.

In Psalm 143, David not only documented his despair, but he showed us how he conversed with God about the paralysis in his life. It's a perfect blueprint for us to follow. David knew that he couldn't stay paralyzed, and he knew that God was the answer.

Read Psalm 143.

While we may not be facing the same kind of threats that David was facing, I think it's safe to say that at some point in our lives, we've all felt afraid like David. Right?

We all have been or will be this intensely paralyzed with fear in some area of our lives. Some of you are feeling that way right now.

Trust me when I say our lives don't have to be at risk to feel this kind of despair. It could be fearing that the loss of a job will put you in financial ruin. The fear that a close relationship that's been severed will never be repaired. The fear that your children are going to face hardships. The list of fears is virtually endless.

But what we learn from David in this Psalm is that we can give that paralysis to God. David decided he couldn't just exist in that situation. Instead, he had trust in God's protection and ability to free him from it. David knew where he needed to turn, and he did so faithfully.

Like you and me, David did not want to stay paralyzed. And we should also emulate how he approached it all—how he turned to God to help him walk again.

The most crucial step that people with physical paralysis take is rehabilitation. Paralyzed people will work as hard as they possibly can to restore function in their lives.

Rehabilitation can be excruciating, grueling, and exhausting. But that does not stop them from using everything in their power to get their lives back to the way it used to be.

They have hope. They fight. And they work as hard as possible to change their circumstances.

So, we should too, right?

I pray that you have not or will never have to endure the journey of physical paralysis. But the journey of psychological paralysis is inevitable. Every one of us has or will experience it.

We all have to carry heavy burdens that affect our ability to move. We are all made to feel powerless to change. We all get stuck.

In the next section, we will walk through the key things that David faithfully allowed God to rehabilitate in him and that God wants to rehabilitate in you.

Revealing Questions

All the paralyzing typos and garbage in our lives needs to go! And now you have the tools to identify that. Take some time to reflect on these questions.

1. Paralysis Analysis

Can you think of some of the "typos" in your life right now? Did you have some profound discoveries as you completed the PORCH exercise and the Fruit of the Spirit tests? How did it make you feel to calculate how long you have been struggling? Did you decide that it's time to make a change? What's something that you can ask God to help you do to take that first step?

2. Fears

As you navigated identifying your fears, did you feel differently about the hope of overcoming those fears knowing that God has you? What fears are you ready to toss aside? What are you going to do to give that to God?

3. Psalm 143

As you read Psalm 143, what stood out to you the most? Did you find yourself focusing more on David's misery or David's tremendous faith in God rescuing him? As you find yourself paralyzed with fear like David, what state of mind do you gravitate to, misery or hope? What verse in this Psalm can you memorize to help you navigate those moments?

WHAT GOD WANTS US TO
REHABILITATE

Control Your Control

So letting your sinful nature control your mind leads
to death. But letting the Spirit control your mind leads
to life and peace.

Romans 8:6

I don't know about you, but every time I hear the word "control," Janet Jackson just starts singing in my head. I totally channel the '80s and my big bangs. I know that you can hear those lyrics in your head right now! C'mon, sing with me!

♪ ♪ ♪ ♪

Preach! Sing it, girl! Exactly how our lives should be, right? Ain't nobody gonna keep me from what I want! Ain't nobody gonna tell me what to do! Ain't nobody body gonna control me!

The fact is, throughout our lives, we are fighting to be in control: from the toddler on the floor banging their feet and fists, to the snot-nosed teenager slamming the door, to the "I'm right" fighting spouse, to the raging mad parent of teenagers, to the stubborn old person sitting on their "I've earned respect" throne.

Whether we admit it or not, for the entire timeframe of our lives, we will be battling control. Control comes in all shapes, sizes, and disguises. And when it comes to removing the paralysis from our lives, the control battle rages in full force.

One of the most incredible things that we can continue to learn from David in Psalm 143 was how he handled control. Or, as I should say, how he *handed over* control.

There are three key areas of control that David mastered:

1. David recognized his life was out of control.
2. David recognized he was powerless to control it.
3. David gave all control to God.

Let that sink in for you. David recognized his life was *out of control* and that he was *powerless to control* it. And then he did what? He *gave up* control to God!

David did not live a Janet Jackson control life at all. David gave all control to God. He did this because he recognized that it was only God who would heal him, protect him, and rescue him from a life paralyzed by fear.

And guess what? God did! Throughout David's life, God protected him, rescued him, and freed him. In fact, David commented when he was near his death in 1 Kings 1:29 that God "has rescued me from every danger."

When David gave up control to God, God never failed him. We too can have a happy ending like David did. But it takes us being a willing participant. It takes us giving up our Janet Jackson-like control.

Instead, Carrie Underwood may have said it best when she sang "Jesus Take the Wheel." We have to stop trusting ourselves to steer our lives. We can't control it all. We can't do it all.

We get to these points in our lives after trying desperately to keep our lives from spiraling out of control that we just lose it. We may collapse. We may fall. We may implode. We may explode.

And being in that place really sucks.

But the reality is that's ultimately where we are supposed to end up.

Why? Because we aren't supposed to be in control of all of it. We fail big time at trying to control it all. In some cases, it makes us lose our ever-lovin' minds!

As David did what we need to do instead of trying to control it all—he gave it to God. In other words, we need to keep our eyes on the cross.

I often wonder why the heck I haven't been able to figure that out myself. When my eyes are on the cross, I'm unstoppable. I feel like I can't be defeated. I feel like no level of pain, suffering, or hardship can stop me. I feel renewed instead of destroyed.

Why then do I eventually turn my eyes away from the cross? Why do I choose to get back on my solo train? Why do I take over trying to control?

Why, when I know I will end up feeling . . .

- defeated,
- alone,
- lost, and
- paralyzed.

Is it because I want sorrow? Um, NO!

Is it because I want pain? Duh, NO!

Is it because I don't believe? Heck, NO!

The answer is I don't know. Chances are, we all really don't know.

But here's the beautiful thing about Jesus Christ: if we fail to recognize that chance to turn to him, we don't miss it for good. We don't ever lose our chances of Jesus' intervention. This isn't a "three strikes, and you're out" kind of deal!

Nope.

We get to turn our eyes to the cross whenever we choose to. However often we choose to.

Endlessly.

When we have accepted Jesus into our lives, his spirit is always with us.

Take a moment to think about something difficult you went through when you were commanding control.

Control Freaks

The subject of control is such a difficult one that you may be considering skipping the rest of this chapter. Wouldn't that just be super controlling of you?

Why do you think the consideration of *giving up* control is a difficult one?

I can tell you why.

Because we are control freaks.

We are! We cannot deny this! You may not see it in yourself, but I promise you, there is something in your life that you are refusing to give up control of.

- Do you insist that everything always go your way?
- Do you not trust someone in your life and constantly check their devices?
- Do you control who your kids can hang out with and get too involved in their lives?
- Do you consider yourself a perfectionist and take over everything because no one else could do it as well as you?
- Do you struggle with trusting people in your life?

What, in your life, are you controlling that you don't need to? Perhaps you are in denial about being a control freak. But I promise you, in some fashion, you are. We all fall into at least one, or both, of the following categories:

- Believing, either knowingly or unknowingly, that our control has the power to perfect the broken things in our lives that we have been unable to change on our own.
- Not recognizing that we have been completely powerless to control the things in our lives that are out of control.

If we truly reflect on both of those statements, we can all agree that we really are control freaks in some way. It's in our nature!

We are women, for crying out loud! Who else is going to get things done right? Lord knows we can't count on the men to do it correctly (a.k.a. our way)! Can I get an amen? (Just kidding . . . kind of.)

Don't get me wrong, there are absolutely some things we do need to control in our lives, like remembering to change our underwear. I once discovered my son hadn't changed his underwear in five days. Five days, people. Beyond disgusting. He clearly failed to control this essential requirement in life. And his classmates likely suffered.

There are plenty of other things that we need to control in our lives too, like sending the kids to school on time, not double booking on our crazy "no time for myself" schedules, oh, and changing our own underwear. I know some of you are wearing the same pair as yesterday . . . admit it!

But seriously, I'm not denying the weighty responsibilities we have. If we aren't in control, who will make sure the house doesn't look like a college frat? Who's going to make sure your child doesn't go to school with Ho Hos, Cheez-Its, and fruit snacks for lunch? Who's going to make sure that doesn't end up being dinner too?

These are all great reasons to have some control in life. The problem lies in the fact that we women take on so much responsibility that we simply forget to stop trying to control it all.

There are things in our life that we can't control—where our control alone is not enough. And that leads to things in our lives spiraling out of control. And eventually, that leads to paralysis.

Think back to the exercise we completed before when you calculated the number of years you've been struggling with your paralysis. What does that tell you?

For most, it is an indication that being on your solo control train is not working out well. It's not enough.

It's time to:

1. Accept that our control of these broken situations is failing.
2. Accept that we are powerless to control the things in our lives that are out of control.
3. Give control of those situations to God.

How to Control Your Control

When I was preparing for this ministry, I got to a point where I was paralyzed in this very spot. I was totally stuck with where to take this message about control and, frankly, avoided writing for a while.

During this timeframe, I decided to attend a women's retreat with ladies from my church. As we were in the chapel that Saturday morning, I was flipping to the verse the speaker had led us to and happened to notice a page in my Bible had been accidentally bent. Being a little superstitious, I thought to myself, "I wonder what God wants me to find on this page." But, since I was tracking with the speaker, I continued to the directed verse and forgot all about the bent page.

Well, fast forward to later in the day. I had gone to the lake to have some much-needed alone time with God. I had a conversation with God that went like this:

Me: What do I need to be working on in my life?

God: Control your control.

Me: Mmkay . . .

I didn't want to hear that business. Our conversation continued, and I asked God specifically about the struggle I was having with writing.

Me: Okay, Lord, I have a problem, I can see the beginning of this book, and I can see the end, but I can't see the in-between.

God: Control your control.

Argh! That was not the answer I was hoping for! I was hoping for an actual answer to my very specific question. But, in typical fashion, God throws this control crap in my face. Bleh.

But I obliged. I went on a mission to try to understand what he was telling me. And the only place I could search for the answer was right where I should have been looking the whole time.

The Bible.

So, I did what any biblical novice does. I jumped in the back of my Bible to the keyword section and looked for the word "control." (Google is equally effective.)

And the first page it directed me to was the random bent page.

Of course, he did!

This is how our amazing, profound, gracious God works. He gives a big old wham, bam, slap-in-the-face moment of his presence that says, "I got somethin' to say to you, woman!"

As it turns out, God was directing me to Romans 7 and 8 crafted by none other than Paul, the former Christian persecutor turned disciple. He wrote it with the intent to share the good news of Jesus Christ with the Romans.

Read Romans 7 and 8.

These chapters in Romans served a very important purpose. *So much good news!*

What can we learn from these chapters that can help us with our control freak tendencies? Let's start with the following two verses:

> *I don't really understand myself, for I want to do what is right, but I don't do it. Instead, I do what I hate.*
>
> ### *Romans 7:15*

> *I want to do what is good, but I don't. I don't want to do what is wrong, but I do it anyway.*
>
> ### *Romans 7:19*

Does this sound familiar to you? Can you relate to how Paul was feeling? I know I can.

It sure seems like Paul was struggling with some control issues, huh? In fact, these passages would indicate that Paul was likely struggling with control issues to the same extent that we are. Paul felt he could control things in his life and do what was right, but ultimately, he was living a life that was out of control! He too was powerless to control the things in his life that were out of control.

God used Paul to demonstrate to the Romans and to all of us who believe in him that even his most loyal disciples struggled with control. They too were paralyzed in the broken areas of their lives.

But that's not all that God wanted you to hear.

Paul also said,

> *I am not the one doing wrong;*
> *it is sin living in me that does it.*

Romans 7:17

> *But if I do what I don't want to do, I am not really the*
> *one doing wrong; it is sin living in me that does it.*

Romans 7:20

Think about the gravity of this passage. In essence, God is telling us that we can't control the paralysis in our lives because the paralysis is controlling us.

It's sin controlling us!

That means *stop beating yourself up* about whatever is out of control in your life. It doesn't define who you are.

You are not a bad person.

You don't have to feel shame.

You don't have to feel guilt.

You don't have to hide.

Why? Because it's not you. You are fearfully and wonderfully made by God our maker. You are God's creation. You are his child. Your life is out of control for one reason and one reason only . . . it's sin.

It's sin!

As we know from when Jesus healed the paralyzed man in Capernaum, this sin that has been controlling you and has you paralyzed has already been washed away, forgiven, and let go through the crucifixion of Jesus Christ. He shed his blood so you don't have to carry that sin anymore. He bore our sin and shame. He took those heavy burdens that are paralyzing you to the cross.

Jesus Christ didn't die so your sins or the sins of others could continue to control you. He didn't suffer an excruciating death on the cross so your sins and the sins of others could continue to paralyze you. He died on the cross to free you.

The Scripture goes on to give the most powerful message:

> *I have discovered this principle of life that when I want to do what is right, I inevitably do what is wrong. I love God's law with all my heart. But there is another power within me that is at war with my mind. This power makes me a slave to the sin that is still within me. Oh, what a miserable person I am! Who will free me from this life that is dominated by sin and death? Thank God! The answer is in Jesus Christ our Lord.*
>
> ### *Romans 7:21–25*

Paul says that we will inevitably fail when we try to control something because of the sin inside us. In other words, we control freaks simply cannot try controlling these things on our own and expect to succeed.

But there is good news! Even when we fail in life to control this sin, through Jesus Christ, we can be freed from it! All those temporary failures you've had? Dismiss them. Jesus frees us.

> *So now there is no condemnation for those who belong to Christ Jesus. And because you belong to him, the power of the life-giving Spirit has freed you from the power of sin that leads to death.*
>
> ### *Romans 8:1–2*

The *power* of the life-giving Spirit has freed us.

> *So letting your sinful nature control your mind leads*
> *to death. But letting the Spirit control your mind leads*
> *to life and peace.*

Romans 8:6

What a fantastic truth to carry with us. The power of God can free us, and that leads us to life and peace. Who doesn't want to have life and peace? We all do, right?

All it takes is training ourselves to let the spirit control our minds instead of our sinful nature, and then we will find it.

So, when it comes to our role as willing participants in giving this control to God, it comes down to our choices.

Remember the signals we talked about? Do we let the outside world, our old ways, or Satan influence our decisions? Or do we instead choose to turn to God?

God tells us in Romans 8:6 that when we let God control—or should I say, when we let "Jesus take the wheel"—that's where we will find peace. And that's when we will be freed from paralysis.

We don't have to be in control to be freed from the paralysis in our lives. Only God does.

I know this is a hard message for you control freaks out there. But give it one big try right now, just like David.

God has this.

Rehabilitation Questions

Giving up control is never an easy process, especially when we don't recognize all the areas where we have unhealthy control. Take some time to reflect on these questions.

1. Control Recognition

Have you been living your life more like Janet Jackson (control freak) or Carrie Underwood (Jesus take the wheel)? Have you identified areas of your life that are out of control? Have you recognized that you have been powerless to control the things paralyzing you in life? Where you in your journey to give control of your battle with paralysis to God?

2. Control Your Control

What steps could you take to begin to transform controlling the things that you should not control? How does it make you feel to recognize that it is sin, not the child of God that you are, that is controlling your broken ways? Does it make you want to boot sin out the door? Confess it and God to take that sin from you.

3. Giving God Control

Is there anything you are dealing with right now that could be easier if you turn your eyes to Jesus? Is hope and peace what you are searching for? Do you think you can achieve hope and peace alone? What would freedom look like for you? Have you asked God for it?

Deter the Fear

"The Lord is my rock, my fortress, and my savior; my God is my rock, in whom I find protection. He is my shield, the power that saves me, and my place of safety. He is my refuge, my savior, the one who saves me from violence. I called on the Lord, who is worthy of praise, and he saved me from my enemies."

2 Samuel 22:2–4

I remember a time when I had just gone back to work after maternity leave with my first born, and his father, being a freelancer, was staying at home with him.

Trying to get back in the game in typical new mother fashion, I worried about my little peanut. It wouldn't be very far into my day before I would try to check in to see how things were going. On that particular day, I tried calling his father at our home for about ten minutes, and he didn't answer the phone.

This was back in the day when we had phones connected to cords. And outlets. Even cell phones were connected to the car. I was living in the dark ages. I could not check Life360. Couldn't check Find My iPhone. No way to check his Snapchat map.

For the ten long minutes that I was trying to get ahold of him, my mind raced into a state of impending doom. My fear was uncontrollable.

In fact, my mind, thanks to the big ol' meanie, had convinced me that he had fallen down in the shower, cracked his head open, was bleeding out, and my little peanut had been screaming for hours unattended. This fear was so vividly true in my mind. It was a reality that I had accepted.

I hopped into my car to race the thirty minutes home to be able to care for my unattended child and his unconscious father. I bawled my brains out the entire way home. I couldn't believe the tragedy that was unfolding.

When I arrived and walked in the front door, I remember the look on my former husband's face as he sat on the couch, shocked that I was bursting through the front door. A "what on Earth are you doing here?" soon followed.

Sure as heck, the ten minutes that I had been calling him, he had been in the shower. Only his head was not cracked opened, and the baby was not unattended and screaming in horror. There was no single ounce of truth to any of the fears that had unfolded in my head.

I'd like to say that this was just a one-time occurrence, but it had already been a trend in my life. It was not until I started writing this book that I recognized just how far back my irrational fears went.

And this behavior would continue throughout the course of my life. My anxiety, irrational fears, and belief in Satan's evil lies would haunt me in all sorts of ways for years to come. This anxiety would eventually lead to paralyzing fears.

But there was a reason Satan was attacking me. He didn't want me to share the fundamental truth that God so desperately wants us to recognize: God does not want us to have fear.

Philippians 4:6–7 will forever be my weapon.

Do not be anxious about anything, but in every situation, with prayer and petition, present your requests to God. And the peace of God, which transcends all understanding, will guard your hearts and your minds in Christ Jesus.

Philippians 4:6–7 NIV

When I say that verse out loud and pray on it to God, he inevitably provides me with peace. Every. Single. Time.

I have to think this was David's thought process too. In Psalm 143, when David was paralyzed with fear as he was under attack, this becomes clear.

You recall, David cried out to the Lord saying,

I am losing all hope; I am paralyzed with fear.

Psalm 143:4

This could have been the end of David's story. He could have resigned to hiding in caves and running in fear for the rest of his life. He could have chosen to never come out of hiding and bail on his anointment as the next king of Israel.

But he didn't.

Instead, he turned to God to lead him from being paralyzed with fear and to move forward.

Let me hear of your unfailing love each morning, for I am trusting you. Show me where to walk, for I give myself to you. Rescue me from my enemies, Lord; I run to you to hide me. Teach me to do your will, for you are my God. May your gracious Spirit lead me forward on a firm footing.

Psalm 143:8–10

The greatest weapon that David used to help him overcome his fears was faith. Faith was his shield. Faith was his armor. Faith was his sword.

David could have cowered for the remainder of his days, hiding in fear. But he didn't. He stepped forward in faith.

The Lord says, "I will rescue those who love me. I will protect those who trust in my name. When they call on me, I will answer; I will be with them in trouble. I will rescue and honor them."

Psalms 91:14–15

I think that is an amazing promise. It sounds a lot like what David was asking for when he wanted God to protect him.

When fear stands alone, it remains just fear. But when we add faith to the equation, fear's hold over us diminishes.

When it comes to getting us to buy into the idea of not being fearful, God overachieved. He tells us 365 times in the Bible to not have fear—365 times, people! That is a reminder for every day of the year.

There's this old rule in marketing that perhaps some of you have heard. The rule essentially states that in order to get somebody to buy into something, you have to tell them seven times. God told us this 365 times! Do you think that God wanted to get that through to us?

My friend Jesse takes this daily reminder to heart now. For a long time, she had no idea how paralyzed with fear she was. For her, it had just become a way of life.

Jesse's social anxiety paralyzed her. She avoided being around people just so she wouldn't have to talk to somebody. She feared rejection. She feared abandonment. She feared being broken by friendships.

When Jesse began to understand how much God did not want her to have fear, it was life changing. She saw that she had a friendship with fear rather than people.

Think about that! How many of us can say that we are friends with fear? Strange perspective, for sure. But when I look at how much time I've spent with fear, you'd think we were best friends! I'm pretty sure fear is the friend that I crack a beer with on the deck and that chooses to stay too long.

When God revealed this to Jesse and she saw fear for what it really is, not a friend but a foe, it opened up her world. She was able to step out in faith and begin to socialize with people. Her faith transformed her. To the point that she was able to stand in a room full of about one hundred women and share that testimony.

Where are you in your journey with fear? Is it paralyzing you? Is fear your friend or your foe?

Faith Over Fear

For the past several years, I've been seeing 11:11 all the time. I see it every day. More often than not, I see it multiple times a day. I see it on clocks, on receipts, in Excel documents, on scoreboards, and various other things. Seeing 11:11 has become a part of my daily existence.

When this started happening, I, of course, thought that it was coincidental—just a fluke. But after a while, I determined this is not accidental. On the contrary, I believe that 11:11 has become quite intentional in my life.

Being the anxious person that I am, in the beginning, these occurrences freaked me out. I was pretty fearful that 11:11 meant something terrible was going to happen to me. I was sure that doom was impending.

In fact, in 2011, I was dreading November 11. These concerns were elevated when I learned that I had to fly to New York for a client meeting on 11/11/11.

When one is anticipating impending doom on a day that has been haunting you every single day for years, air travel is not ideal for the nerves.

It was pretty much a poop-my-pants feeling I experienced that whole day. It was paralyzing. I remember praying fervently that the wheels would land and that God would let me live a few more years here on this great Earth.

As you know, I survived that flight. Those numbers did not take me down. Instead, it may have given me a great gift. What I realized on that day is that I had to stop looking at my life with a sense of impending doom. That perhaps, I needed to start looking at 11:11 and my life differently.

I started coming to grips with the fact that maybe it wasn't a sign that something terrible was going to happen to me. Perhaps, it was a sign that something wonderful was going to happen to me.

Where I turned to next to find an answer to my 11:11 predicament was where I should have turned to in the first place, the Bible.

At this stage in 2011, while my faith was strong, my exposure to the Bible was mostly limited to reading a few chapters infrequently. And honestly, I comprehended very little of it. I wanted to know more and learn the stories within the Bible, but I did not have the discipline to take enough time to learn it.

So, imagine me, this clueless Bible seeker, thumbing through the Bible to find my 11:11 answer. It happened to lead me to Hebrews 11.

Now some of you may or may not know the significance of this chapter. I think it's one of the most profound chapters in the Bible. It's essentially the faith hall of fame. One could also call it "Bible Faith Stories Cliff Notes" or "Bible Faith for Dummies." Whatever you want.

Seventeen acts of faith are highlighted in this chapter, starring some of the best-known faith warriors in the Bible: Abel, Enoch, Noah, Abraham, Sarah, Isaac, Jacob, Joseph, Moses, the people of Israel, and Rahab. And appearing in supporting roles were Gideon, Barak, Samson, Jephthah, David, Samuel, and all the prophets.

Read Hebrews 11.

Here is a highlight of what these warriors did in the name of faith:

> *By faith these people overthrew kingdoms, ruled with justice, and received what God had promised them. They shut the mouths of lions, quenched the flames of fire, and escaped death by the edge of the sword. Their weakness was turned to strength. They became strong in battle and put whole armies to flight. Women received their loved ones back again from death.*
>
> *But others were tortured, refusing to turn from God in order to be set free. They placed their hope in a better life after the resurrection. Some were jeered at, and their backs were cut open with whips. Others were chained in prisons. Some died by stoning, some were sawed in half, and others were killed with the sword. Some went about wearing skins of sheep and goats, destitute and oppressed and mistreated. They were too good for this world, wandering over deserts and mountains, hiding in caves and holes in the ground.*

> ***Hebrews 11:33–38***

I imagine you read that with the same "What the . . ." reaction I did. My gosh, did they face some fear! Tremendous fear! These people clearly faced the impossible. If you are like me, these incredible feats seem like something that you or I could never face or endure.

But they did. When it comes to what paralyzes us with fear, we will too.

I know what it feels like to face the impossible. Several times in my life, I've felt chained in prison. I've felt like I was facing a lion. And I've felt like I was facing the edge of a sword. And I'm certain that you have too.

When you think about what has you paralyzed in your life, does it seem any less impossible? Does the thought of facing your fears or changing them seem any easier?

If you are anything like me, the answer is no! They feel impossible. The fear is too substantial.

What these people in the Bible faced physically is what we feel emotionally. These people had fear just like you and I do. But this did not paralyze them. They had the tool to overcome those fears.

Faith.

They knew that even though they faced death, imprisonment, and pain, they had faith that God would help them prevail. They even had to deal with the fears of people thinking they were absolutely nuts. But that didn't stop them from believing that it was all possible. They had total and complete faith in God's promises.

Hebrews 11 brings us one of the most powerful verses in the Bible about faith:

> *Faith shows the reality of what we hope for; it is the evidence of things we cannot see.*
>
> ### *Hebrews 11:1*

You have likely heard the term "blind faith." It comes from this verse. The truth is faith is always blind. It's a given. Only God can see what's ahead. When we have confidence in what God promises us, our faith is blind.

Blind faith is what Jesus loved about the Roman officer who came to him to heal his paralyzed servant. Do you remember what played out here? Let's recap.

But the officer said, "Lord, I am not worthy to have you come into my home. Just say the word from where you are, and my servant will be healed."

Matthew 8:8

Think about the level of faith the Roman officer had at this moment. He was essentially saying to Jesus, "I trust you with the impossible. I don't need you to be present to heal my servant; I believe that *your words*, right here and right now, can heal him." This Roman officer not only believed in the miracle but had faith in Jesus' incredible power to *heal with words*.

The Roman officer wasn't a disciple. They weren't pals. In fact, it's widely believed that he had never even crossed paths with Jesus himself but had just heard about him. Yet, the Roman officer still had this tremendous blind faith that Jesus could heal his servant with just his words. This had a significant impact on Jesus.

When Jesus heard this, he was amazed. Turning to those who were following him, he said, "I tell you the truth, I haven't seen faith like this in all Israel!"

Matthew 8:10

Jesus was so blown away by this that he gave the Roman officer the recognition of "Greatest Faith in all of Israel." Think about the magnitude of that being given that recognition from Jesus Christ himself. Consider all the faithful people who walked before him like John the Baptist, who declared Jesus as "the Lamb of God, who takes away the sin of the world" (John 1:29) and his disciples who left everything and followed him, just to name a few.

Despite these tremendous acts of faith by Jesus' followers, this Roman officer, who was likely a less-than-stellar human, won this reward from Jesus Christ.

Jesus constantly surprises me by how much he loves and admires us regular folk. How much he rewards us despite all our baggage. And how much he still leads us despite our failures.

What also surprises me is how spot-on he always is. When he tells us to not worry and trust that he will make a way, he will make a way. When he tells us to not be anxious about anything, he means *anything*. And when he says to not have fear and have faith in his protection, he follows through.

My faith walk changed when I made the decision to blindly walk with God and trust him so I don't have fear. I still see 11:11 to this day, and it serves as a reminder to me to continue to have blind faith. Find something in your life that can be your reminder to blindly trust God in your walk every single day.

Waves of Fear

Just over a year ago, I invested in myself. And I'm not talking about a trip to the mall to buy some fantastic boots and clothes. I'm talking about investing in time to help me on my spiritual and professional walk.

If this is something that you don't do on occasion, I highly, highly encourage it. Tell your boss, hubby, significant other, parents, or whoever has a say in what you do that I command that you to. Who will argue with that, right?

I love, love, love the ocean: the sunshine, the water, the sand, all of it. And the biggest reason why is because God always talks to me there.

When I got the offer to attend a one-day mastermind retreat in Los Angeles, I shot my hand up, waving it around like a grade-schooler who was about to wet their pants. "Take me, take me now!"

But I didn't just sign up for one day. I took a day before and a day after to just be on my own. I needed time to pray, reflect, and just be alone with God.

It was well worth it.

The last day I was there, I headed to the beach for a stroll. And like most, I found myself just watching the world do its thing.

It started off with just watching some folks attempting to swim out in the ocean. Attempting is the key word here. They had to remain pretty close to shore because the ocean was roaring that day. Each wave was knocking them off their feet—every whitecap exhausting them. And every attempt to make progress out to sea was blocked by a force far more powerful than they were. They stood no chance. And frankly, if they were a little less careful, they could have been the ocean's victim that day. The waves were pummeling them and pummeling them hard.

It made me think about how difficult life can sometimes feel—like a big wave crashing upon us.

This is what it felt like for me and so many others when the coronavirus pandemic started to sweep across our globe, just a few weeks after I stood on that beach.

I know several like me have felt like they were getting pummeled, just like these swimmers. But instead of ocean waves, we were pummeled by fear. By uncertainty. By the major changes to our lives. No doubt, for some of us, it felt like giant waves crashing right on top of us again and again.

To me, the virus felt like a tremendous force far more powerful than we were. It seemed like it managed to inhibit the progress of the entire human race. And no doubt, it literally knocked our nation and our world off its feet.

I realize that for some, they handled the pandemic without fear. And I wished so badly that I was one of them. But for me, I was fearful. This hypochondriac—this doomsday-dreader—she struggled.

I had moments of forgetting my faith. Moments of forgetting to trust. And moments of forgetting to lean into the One who was far more powerful than this virus.

And there were moments when I felt like I was taking on a big, giant wave alone.

I found myself desperately trying to control everything. Every hand wash, wipe down, Lysol spray, Clorox wipe, mask, and glove was an obsessive attempt to prevent my family from being taken under and falling victim to that powerful force. Every headline, social media post, and press conference of doom and gloom exhausted me and had me questioning my ability to stay afloat.

There's no doubt there were days when the coronavirus wave made me feel like I was drowning.

But then God revealed to me the next part of the story on the beach in LA. Just beyond the swimmers who were barely staying afloat was a group of surfers. The groups of surfers on their surfboards were taking on the very same waves as the swimmers. Only their battle with the same waves looked quite different. Actually, it didn't look like a battle at all.

The surfers had no fear as they took the waves head-on. Their anxiety: non-existent. They had something to carry them over the wave. In fact, that something actually made the wave feel like a smooth ride. It would keep them afloat no matter how big of a wave was coming at them. And no matter what, progress was made as they ventured deeper into the rough sea.

That's what it was like when I decided to bring God into my battle with the tidal wave of coronavirus, and the tidal wave of Todd's accident, and the tidal wave with my codependency, and so on.

Every time I invited God into the process, it would start to feel less like a battle and more like a ride. Taking the anxiety, fear, and dread crashing down upon me and turning it into a smooth ride of hope, trust, and faith.

There are two things that we can take to the bank:

1. The waves we face in life don't change, but how we navigate them does.
2. When God is our surfboard, we do not have to fear the waves we are taking on.

In the moments that I've turned to him and trusted, I've felt carried. I've felt taken care of. I've felt like I could surrender the burden of control I've been carrying. I've felt completely and totally protected.

There is no doubt that the coronavirus (as well as every battle we have faced and will face) was a big, powerful force. But in comparison to the power that God has, it is minuscule. God is far more powerful than we can possibly imagine and a bigger force than anything that has ever existed.

And that power is the very same power he placed within us through the Holy Spirit when we accepted him into our lives. When we use the power that he placed within us, we can navigate these rough waters very differently. We don't get pummeled; we glide over it.

And like surfers, our focus stops being about this giant wave taking us out; instead, it's about what is beyond it. We stop having fears and start having faith.

What would it do for you if you were to change this perspective right now? How would your heart, mind, and soul feel if you were focused beyond the paralyzing waves in your life and look at what is beyond it?

If instead of fear, you could have hope, trust, and faith in what is in front of you? What peace would that bring to your life?

As I looked beyond the waves crashing onshore, the rest of the ocean came into view. It was not a raging sea. It was calm. It was peaceful. It went on forever. It was beautiful. It looked like what our salvation looks like. Perfect. No more scary waves. Just smooth sailing.

When we understand the incredible beauty and perfection of salvation, the fear of our own death begins to dissipate. When we turn to hope and trust in God, the fear of overcoming paralysis begins to subside. And when we lean on our faith and pray hard, the fear of what the future holds disappears.

Rehabilitation Questions

Fear is often the biggest factor in being psychologically paralyzed. But God desires most for us to have faith over fear. Take some time to reflect on these questions.

1. Fear

When you look at the things paralyzing you in your life, what fears do you have? Have you taken the step to give those fears to God? What steps can you take to turn your fear over to God and trust that he will protect you?

2. Faith

Where are you in your faith walk with God? Are you in a position of following him blindly? Are you confident in him protecting you? Do you think you are capable of waking up every day and reminding yourself of his daily promise to not have fear?

3. Navigating Waves of Fear

How smooth have the waves you have faced in life been? How do you want to take on future waves in your life? Do you want to cower in fear at the coming waves? Or do you want to say, "COWABUNGA," and experience a smoother ride?

Step by Misstep

Though they stumble, they will never fall,
for the Lord holds them by the hand.

Psalms 37:24

As Jesus called the Paralyzed man in Capernaum to "rise up and walk," there was an expectation that the man would do as He commanded. He expected that man to walk and take a stroll. Think for a second about what that moment looked like. If I were to venture a guess, that man didn't walk perfectly as He stood. His legs that had not been used likely didn't have much muscle structure or stability. And as a result, I'm confident that he probably had a few missteps as he got his bearings.

Now imagine if that man stopped dead in his tracks after his missteps. Imagine him plopping himself down on his mat and deciding to stay paralyzed. What would have become of this powerful story? Jesus forgives a man of his sins and heals him of paralysis, and the dude says, "Yeah, thanks. I suck, sorry, but I'm going to stay right here. Thanks anyway." Would that story even have made it in the New Testament?

I think not.

Thank goodness, he did not do that. The dude did not return to his paralyzed state. Instead, he stepped by his missteps.

Unfortunately, our track records are often not as good. We tend to struggle to step by our missteps. Too often, we choose to give up and stay paralyzed when we have temporary failures.

Do you realize that when we do this, we are essentially saying to Jesus, "Yeah, I suck, so I'm going to stay right here, thanks though"?

Imagine if King David had had this mindset. We know that David was known for his faith in God. He was known as "a man after God's own heart" because of his devotion to the Lord.

But David was also an incredible sinner, perhaps one of the worst among God's most faithful servants. First, he took advantage of another man's wife, Bathsheba. But then it gets worse. He also had her husband, Uriah, murdered—a guy who was actually defending David's throne. Seriously, this is as bad of a misstep as things can get. He was Naughty Naughterson!

You would think that David would not have been able to recover from such a hardened heart. That he would have been entirely unfit to ever serve the Lord again. But David acknowledged his sin, falling to his knees and humbling himself before God, and the Lord forgave him.

> *David said to Nathan, "I have sinned against the Lord."*
> *And Nathan said to David, "The Lord also has put away*
> *your sin; you shall not die."*
>
> ### *2 Samuel 12:13 ESV*

I'm not sharing this to give you any ideas of taking someone out, of course. But put yourself in David's shoes at this moment. Would you have been able to accept God's forgiveness? Would you have been able to continue doing God's work? Would you have been able to step by your missteps?

Don't kid yourself. David's sins didn't come without consequence. He suffered a great deal of pain as a result of it. His son betrayed him, he was abused, one son killed another, he received death threats—his life did not get easier.

You would think that the shame of his missteps would have left him paralyzed with grief and regrets. That the consequences of his sin would have had him living in constant fear. And his shame would have led to feelings of a loss of purpose. One would think for all these reasons, he would have been unable to step by these missteps.

And while David surely felt all those feelings significantly, he did not stay paralyzed by them. Instead, David chose to face them with hope and faith in God. He lived by believing in God's promises. His hope is captured well in Psalm 145:

> *The Lord always keeps his promises; he is gracious in all he does. The Lord helps the fallen and lifts those bent beneath their loads.*
>
> ### Psalm 145:13–14

David acknowledged that God had forgiven him for his missteps, and he had hope in continuing to step forward. And he also knew that God wanted to use his missteps for good. He stepped by his missteps to continue ministering for the Lord.

> *Restore to me the joy of your salvation and grant me a willing spirit, to sustain me. Then I will teach transgressors your ways, so that sinners will turn back to you . . . Open my lips, Lord, and my mouth will declare your praise.*
>
> ### Psalm 51:12–13, 15 NIV

How'd the decision to move past the sins that could have paralyzed him for life turn out for him? How'd his commitment to serving the Lord after failing him so significantly play out for him?

> *So David son of Jesse reigned over all Israel. He reigned over Israel for forty years, seven of them in Hebron and thirty-three in Jerusalem. He died at a ripe old age, having enjoyed long life, wealth, and honor.*
>
> ### 1 Chronicles 29:26–28

David died enjoying life, living with wealth, and having honor. Seriously, people, his adulterer. This murderer. This super-naughty but God-loving man died living the good life.

I'm not suggesting by any means that if you freely go out and do any of the above, you are going to make it rain later in life. But I am suggesting that whatever you do that hangs you up should never keep you from moving forward. You too should step by your missteps.

There is nothing that can keep you from God's forgiveness if you have accepted him into your heart. There is nothing that can keep you from having hope in his promises. There is nothing that can keep you paralyzed by the mistakes you've made.

Our Blooper Reel

I like to think of our lives as a movie in the making. It takes a long time to make and a whole lot of takes to finally get it right. But the outcome is just as the director planned.

Our lives are produced in a similar way. The vision God has for us is perfectly crafted over time into what he plans for our lives. It takes a long time to create and a whole lot of takes.

The challenge we have is that our mindsets are different than our Creator. Instead of focusing on the beautiful movie that is being created in our lives, we get caught up in the blooper reel: every slip-up, misstep, and mistake reels in our minds. We forget about the good takes and can't get past the bad. Our lives feel like a whole life of bloopers—and not the funny kind.

But here's what happens to bloopers in the movie-making process. They get edited out. They don't make the final cut. They aren't the finished product.

So, why aren't we editing out the bloopers in our lives? Why do we let it be part of the final product of what we view in our lives?

I don't know about you, but I despise movies that have horrible things continuing to go wrong for the main character—like in the movie, *Meet the Parents*. For those of you familiar with the movie and its perhaps "colorful" tone, please show me some grace for this reference.

In this movie, everything under the sun goes wrong for Ben Stiller's character, Greg. His character goes to meet the parents of his fiancé. The father, played by Robert De Niro, ends up hating his guts. Everything that Greg does in this movie is disastrous. It's beyond painful to watch.

I give it a splat on my tomato meter. Not because the acting sucked or there wasn't humor in it. In fact, this movie was hilarious and an incredible hit. But I struggled with it because watching pain happen to someone over and over and over again is not enjoyable to me in any way, shape, or form. Barf.

But wow, when I ask myself what kind of movie reel of my own life I tend to watch on repeat (you know the type of movie you have memorized), it's clear that it is the same kind of painful movie that *Meet the Parents* feels like to me. Watching pain happen to me over and over and over again. Barf.

Do you feel my pain?

When we can step by our missteps and edit out the parts of our lives where we made mistakes, we gain greater wisdom. Rather than wallowing in the poor decisions we have made and continue to make, we learn from them. We recognize how to step around them when they rear their ugly heads again in the future. And most importantly, we can move forward.

Take Rebecca, who, after twenty years of being in an abusive relationship, was able to find freedom. Well, in true big ol' meanie fashion, Satan, of course, tried to sink his claws back into her.

In her first relationship since her divorce, she found herself with the same kind of man—with the same controlling and potentially abusive behaviors.

The game changer for her this time was the wisdom she had gained. God had taught her to think differently, and he transformed her heart. As soon as she was able to recognize the unhealthy behavior, she turned from it. The Holy Spirit was on guard for her and empowered her to be bold and brave and walk from it. Again.

Rebecca went on to find the man of her dreams. She describes him as kind, loving, and an answer to her prayers. Her perspective no longer focuses on the blooper reel of her broken life but on the good life that she is living.

So, what about you? What bloopers of your life do you keep watching over and over again? What missteps in your life are you unable to step by? Can you instead find the wisdom that God has taught you along the way?

Find a way to capture that wisdom and watch it on repeat. Memorize it. And when you are ready, go a step more and teach it. God will use it in amazing ways.

Their Missteps

Paralysis doesn't just exist when we are unable to step by our own missteps. If we are being honest with ourselves, we take issue with others' lives, not just our own. Our inability to step by the missteps of others is a misstep of ourselves. In fact, it's a cultural paralysis we are all living in. We are sinning by judging the sins of others.

Let me share an example.

We all have those women in our lives that we just do not like. You know who I'm talking about. They may appear rude, better than you, or plain, well, bitchy. They are the ones we gossip to our friends about, the ones we go out of our way to avoid, and the ones that, for some reason, we think are much less likable than ourselves.

We are, after all, likable. Right?

Or are we?

It took me a few years of being friends with my besties before I found out the truth—and it was a truth that was pretty tough for me to swallow. I discovered that before my best friends really knew me, they thought that I was the b-word. (From here on out, I'll just call myself a "B.")

This blew me away. These were my best friends, and I couldn't imagine that I had ever come across as a B. While I definitely crossed the B-line on several occasions when I was too cocky in my early career, I felt that I had a pretty different persona in public and in my community. In fact, I thought that I had always been friendly to people, and I constantly had a smile on my face. I was outgoing and not shy by any means. In my mind, although I had a tendency to be assertive, I thought that people would consider me pretty doggone nice!

But my perception of who I was, was not the girl that was being seen. I was seeing the outside person that I thought I was . . . and they were seeing my inside. And the inside girl was not smiling. The inside girl simply couldn't.

One of my friends said I would come in to pick up my son from preschool, all fancy dressed up in my suit and heels, and would grab my kid and go. I would not socialize with the teachers or get to know them. I would just jet-set out of there as fast as I could.

Another one of my friends said that I would constantly blow her off when trying to get to know me and connect with our children. She would see me at the gym and say, "We really need to get our sons together for a play date," and I would say, "That's a great idea!" and then she would never hear from me again.

I'm sure there are countless other examples I could share. And many stories that have never been shared with me.

But what my friends have realized since they have gotten to know me is that the girl that they thought was being a B, wasn't intentionally being a B at all. She was exhausted. She was distracted. And she was completely overwhelmed.

I was so unaware that they had that perception of me because I was living a life that was completely unaware of things around me. I didn't have the capacity for it. I was burning the candle at every end possible. I was living in survival mode and in a fog. And that is what they saw.

Personally, I can tell you that my life was a blur. To give you an idea of my mental state, Todd (before we were together) was my children's Little League coach . . . and I couldn't have told you his name. I didn't give him the time of day. Crappy of me, right?

But it wasn't intentional. I just couldn't see outside of what was consuming me inside. My life was a complete fog. I remember running in my heels to the ball diamond so I wouldn't miss another game. And then just collapsing in a heap in the stands. Even mustering up a conversation with my good friend felt next to impossible.

I share this story with you because this story is not just my own. It is the story of so many. Women are tired. Women are stressed. Women are paralyzed in pain.

And women need grace.

As this situation played out for me, it really made me start to think about the mental state of women. I started thinking about the women that I've thought were a B. The ones that seemed to blow me off. The ones that seemed to hate me. And that's when I realized, perhaps none of that is really true. Maybe they too are tired.

I mean, who would really set out to be a B? Who makes that their life mission? Who would ever want to be known as that?

The more realistic situation is that the women we see in this light in our life are going through something. Perhaps their marriage is struggling. Maybe they are concerned they might lose their job. Perhaps their baby woke them up every fifteen minutes the night before. There are so many things in life that are taxing, and we can't expect every woman to handle it with a Stepford Wives smile. Some women just can't help but have their inside show on the outside.

That's where we come in. We could be the difference in their life. We could be the grace that they need.

Finally, all of you should be of one mind. Sympathize with each other. Love each other as brothers and sisters.

1 Peter 3:8

Imagine the next time you see someone being a B, actually stopping and saying a prayer for whatever they are dealing with. Imagine what that grace could do for them. Imagine what that grace would do for *you*. It could be life changing for all involved.

That's what my friends did. At one point in time, one friend actually said to her husband, "I'm going to get her." She didn't want to write me off. She wanted to reach me. And she is now one of my dearest friends, my warrior, and my sister in Christ. I did not have that kind of spiritual connection with friends prior to these women. Their persistence in stepping by my missteps changed the course of my life.

So, next time you come across a B, my challenge to you is to not complain or be a B back. Back her up. Pray for her. Be kind to her. Give her grace—step by her misstep.

God's View of Our Missteps

Sometimes, I think one of the most challenging parts of moving past our paralysis is our perception of what God thinks of our missteps. Our fear of his judgment paralyzes us with guilt and shame.

But one thing is truly clear in the Bible. God has mercy on us. It's the entire reason and existence of Jesus Christ walking on Earth. He was sacrificed for the same.

> *"For this is how God loved the world: He gave his one and only Son, so that everyone who believes in him will not perish but have eternal life."*
>
> ### *John 3:16*

No matter how far we've wandered. No matter how much we've rebelled. No matter how big we've failed. God has mercy on us.

When he sent his Son to die for our sins, God was stepping past our missteps. Period.

God doesn't have a trash bin to throw us away or a rejection letter to send. God simply doesn't give up on us. He rescues us.

This has got to be one of the biggest battles we all deal with: not feeling worthy of God's love because of our missteps. Feeling like a throw-away. *Who on Earth would want to save me? I'm just a big old pile of poo who keeps failing, running, and disobeying.*

But imagine God's argument to that! "Woman, do you know the mercy I've shown you? Do you know the grace I've provided you? Do you know the sacrifice I made for you? Get over your missteps. I've got it handled!"

Ponder how Paul must have felt with all his missteps. Paul, formerly Saul, literally persecuted Christians. He was a Pharisee who despised followers of Jesus and was trying to destroy the church of God. He literally went from house to house, dragging men and women off to prison and called for them to be stoned.

Tell me right now, don't you think that would be the misstep of all missteps in God's eyes?

I'd say!

But Paul did not let this misstep paralyze him. He used it! He was converted, and he shouted Christianity from the rooftops. God made him a minister, and his witness was instrumental in growing the Christian church. In fact, fourteen of the twenty-seven books in the New Testament are Paul's witness to the life and death of Jesus Christ.

It wasn't easy for him. He had struggles. But Paul led a life of leaving his past behind to serve God and the Christian church. He wasn't concerned that God had not stepped by his missteps. He knew that God was using it!

Brothers, I do not consider that I have made it my own.
But one thing I do: forgetting what lies behind and
straining forward to what lies ahead, I press on toward
the goal for the prize of the upward call of God in
Christ Jesus.

Philippians 3:13–14 ESV

God tells us the very same thing with our missteps. It's behind you. You get to leave it there. You don't have to worry.

Step by it.

Rehabilitation Questions

Jesus died on the cross for a very important reason, to take the missteps of his believers with him. Not so his believers would continue to reel over and be paralyzed by them. Take some time to reflect on these questions.

1. Your Missteps

What missteps play over and over again in your mind? How are those missteps paralyzing you? What could you do to edit out these bloopers in your life? What role will you let God play in that process?

2. Other's Missteps

What interactions do you have with people on a regular basis that makes you view them in hateful ways? What past missteps by others have you not been able to step past? How would Jesus want you to handle these situations, with grace?

3. God's View of Your Missteps

What in your life do you fear God is not stepping past? What paralyzes you because of the shame you feel with God? What steps can you take with God to step by it?

Refocus Your Focus

Set your minds on things that are above,
not on things that are on earth.

Colossians 3:2 ESV

When I think about the focus issues I've had in life, I realize that they started a long time ago. In fact, I think back to the days of College Amanda—my affectionate name for my wild-child college self.

For example, in my first semester in college, I got a GPA of 1.48. Yes, you are reading that right—a 1.48. Granted, I was majoring in engineering, and that was super hard. I'll give myself that. Calculus, physics, and other weed-out engineering courses were on my plate, so it wasn't exactly a semester that I expected to knock out of the park. I was a smart kid, but not one that just gets it. I have to work for it. I have to focus on it.

But getting a 1.48? That was my fault and my fault alone.

College Amanda had plans other than focusing on schoolwork. I had sorority events to attend. Fraternities to hang out at. Dorm besties to drink with *every single day*. Seriously, my focus habits, pretty much non-existent.

The result? Basically failure.

Fortunately, at the time, my college didn't give you the boot. Instead, they gave a grace semester. That grace eventually led me to successfully graduating from that engineering school.

But getting there required me to change my ways. I had to find some focus. And overcome my FOMO. For those of you who don't know what FOMO stands for, it is *fear of missing out*. In college, it's safe to say that I was paralyzed by FOMO. Ms. College Amanda Party Pants could not miss out on a party. That usually led to making stupid decisions including skipping classes, missing homework assignments, and making other poor decisions in life.

As the threat of being booted from my sorority for my less-than-stellar grades loomed, I realized I had to buckle down and find my focus. For me, this meant that I had to get better at the following three things:

1. Distractions—removing them
2. Discernment—improving it
3. Doing—not avoiding it

The best way that I found I could do all three of these was by going off into a quiet area of the sorority house, playing some Mozart on my Walkman, and opening up my books.

I can remember this process vividly. Frankly, it's one of the few things I can remember about the academic part of college. I think the rest of it was so traumatic for me, I've blocked it from my mind. Except for the nightmares I still have to this day of showing up to a test and realizing I never attended the class . . . still haunts me.

But this process of having discernment, minimizing my distractions, and doing what needed to get done worked for me. In fact, I recall pulling an all-nighter one night preparing for an ergonomics test. I escaped all the FOMO temptations. Despite being grossly behind in the class, I managed to memorize every movement that the body makes. And subsequently, I scored very well on the test.

Finally. Success.

This is what it takes in the process of overcoming our paralysis as well. We can't keep living a life of distraction, wrong choices, and procrastination and expect anything to change. We have to find focus—the kind of focus that God would want from us.

David's poetic cry out to God in Psalm 143 shows how he did this.

Let me hear of your unfailing love each morning,
for I am trusting you. Show me where to walk,
for I give myself to you.

Psalm 143:8

This verse demonstrates that David was daily going to God. He wasn't dabbling in God. He wasn't checking in with God only on Sundays.

He was going to God and seeking his guidance daily.

There is no doubt in my mind that the most incredible seasons I've had in life were when I was with God daily. Whether life was good or sucked. They were seasons where I felt I had direction, hope, and trust beyond what I could imagine.

But man, I wish I could tell you that it's all been smooth sailing for me. The same focus issues I had as College Amanda still exist. I still fall into the temptation to chase squirrels. I still make poor decisions when I know better. I still procrastinate with anything important.

But just like my college showed grace for my failures, thank God, he does too. He doesn't give you the boot. You always have the opportunity to succeed in his class.

He will also teach you how. He's not just going to send you home with the textbook and wish you well. In daily communication, he's going to tutor you. He's going to ensure your success.

That's how he's taught me how to approach it. I can refocus on him. He will pause me and redirect me when I'm distracted. He will warn me in the middle of making a bad decision. He will excite me to get moving when I'm feeling unable to move.

When it comes to focusing, I can tell you that this is the hardest out of all the subjects we cover in the book because this is the one where we are accountable. And that can be very difficult for us stubborn humans.

So, work with me here, okay? Choose to put away your distractions and work on these next three sections.

Distractions

We've talked a lot so far about the impact that squirrel chasing has on our walks. When life needs to be directed on the right course, Satan will dangle squirrels in front of you to veer you off course. His mission is to keep you paralyzed.

There is one common squirrel tactic that Satan is using globally that he is having tremendous success with: electronic devices.

The widespread issue paralyzing our world right now is our addiction to devices. The need for our constant interaction with them is a powerful vice that is crippling our ability to be present every day and productive in our life's mission. They, in some cases, have become our God. Glorified and worshipped. Daily sacrifices of our time laid at its feet.

If there has been one huge struggle to finishing this book, it has been my phone. It's like chocolate. If it's in front of me, I have to eat it. I'm sure many of you can all relate to me when I say that it's almost become robotic. I can grab that thing and start scrolling through all my apps without even realizing it. It's like I enter a phone coma. Next thing you know, I wake up, and it's two hours later. And all I got out of it was three more things in my Amazon cart and a whole lot more bitterness and dread. Two hours of lost life!

I think it's hard to make the case that phones have made the world a better place. They have perhaps made the world an easier place. Easier to find stuff, do stuff, communicate stuff for sure. But also, easier to chase stuff, argue, hate, spend, and waste our stinking time. Our phones have become the epicenter of distraction. And sin.

I mean it when I say that. I realize there can be some good stuff that comes out of devices. I use mine for devotions. I contribute to GoFundMe's. I use a prayer app. Some good stuff for sure. But three-quarters of the time (or more), that phone is a distraction. And from what?

The very things that God wants me to focus on.

Think about the things that God wants you to focus on. Is it spending time repairing a broken relationship? Is it walking for thirty minutes a day to help with a health issue? Is it doing some homework so you can fulfill the purpose he has for you? Is it facing the hard steps you need to take to overcome your paralyzing burden from your past?

What are the things he wants you to be focusing on right now? Ask yourself, is your phone stealing your time from doing it?

I guarantee you it is. In fact, I brought this very subject up recently at my Bible study. Every. Single. One of us. Not a soul in the room who wasn't battling this issue. The struggle is real.

I'm not going to tell you that a phone is sinful, aside from the fact that on the back of iPhones, there happens to be a symbol that represents the first sin that ever took place (a bite out of a piece of fruit). Let that sink in. The device attached to our faces literally has the symbolism of sin on it. Yes, take a look for yourself.

It's important to recognize, the phone itself is not sinful but the behavior that it encourages is. And I guarantee you that Satan uses his power to suck you into as much as he can. And right now, I think he is winning.

Our phones cause us to sin in so many ways. They can distract us from being the loving, attentive caretakers we are called to be. They can cause us to fight and hate people over social media. They can create a playground of sexual sin and immorality. They can steal time away from our responsibilities and the things we are called to do. And the list goes on and on and on.

Let's face it, our phones are paralyzing. And they are paralyzing our progress of overcoming the paralyzing burdens in our life. And that can't be good. Something has to change.

I don't know if you've done this before, but you can drill down on your device to see where your screen time has been spent. I, of course, justified my excessive screen time usage as screen time spent for work. "I'm just busy checking emails and texts for work." And it's true, I do spend plenty of time using my device for work-related things. But when I drilled down into the screen time analytics, it told me a very different story. It told me that I was wasting about thirty hours a week on social media.

Seriously. Thirty hours. Of scrolling social media. I about puked seeing the number. I was in shock. You see, I don't sit down for hours on social media. It's sporadic. I might be waiting at a stoplight, in the bathroom, on a boring Zoom call, or trying to sleep. But the reality is that time adds up! To a whopping thirty hours a week. That's almost a full-time job.

I can deny this addiction until the cows come home, but the reality is my device is paralyzing me. It has kept me from writing this book. It keeps me from my prayer and meditation time with God. It keeps me from giving my family my full attention. To sum it up, it keeps me from fulfilling my God-given purpose.

Don't get me wrong. There are good things that can come from our devices. But the truth is that the sin creeps in when we are on them. We might pursue inappropriate relationships or sabotage our important ones. We might think we are learning about how to be a good parent while ignoring actually being one. We might write words for hours, but not one word has a meaningful impact on someone else's life. The list could go on and on.

You too know your struggle with your device. Deep down inside, you know what is keeping you from growing. You know how it's paralyzing you. And you know your God-given purpose is reliant on you chilling out with how much time you spend on it.

One of the biggest areas that devices impact our walk with God is during prayer time. Our devices are reducing our ability to give God our full attention. In fact, according to a study from the Microsoft Corporation, since the start of the mobile revolution, the average attention span has dropped to eight seconds. That's right, eight seconds! According to a popular quote in *Time* magazine, we officially "have a shorter attention span than a goldfish."

Yikes. That's pretty scary. And pretty true! The struggle is real. Do you feel it?

I don't know how many times I've been in prayer, and within a matter of seconds, I have drifted off into Never Never Land. I will be praising God in one second and planning dinner a few seconds later. I will be asking God for forgiveness one minute and then reliving my sins for the next fifteen minutes. I will pray for healing for people for a few minutes and then repeat the same prayer shortly after that because I forgot where I was.

Do you relate to this? Are you struggling with being totally present with God during your prayer time? Do you find yourself drifting over and over again?

If so, your devices could be the reason.

Think back to how people would pray back in biblical times. Fully intentional, invested with heart and mind, attentive toward God. If you need help visualizing what this looked like, go read one or all of the Psalms. These poetic psalms describe how prayer was done—how prayer should be done.

David didn't have Instagram distracting him. He had God distracting him. He didn't have people to argue with on social media. He had God to hand his battles to. He didn't have Words with Friends consuming his every minute. He had his words with God.

Think about the difference this made for him. Being able to fully invest his heart, mind, and soul into his time with God. He was able to overcome battling Goliath, murder attempts, and betrayals, just to name a few.

So, where do we go from here?

The first step, of course, is recognizing that we have a problem. We have to recognize it and start looking at it for what it is—a sinful distraction.

We have to make the decision to start to change this area of our life. Jesus wants your attention. He wants your focus—hold that—he doesn't just want it, he needs it. He needs you to be present with him. He needs you to start listening to him. He needs you to overcome your paralyzing burdens so you can fulfill the purpose he has for you. So do it. Unbury your nose from your phone. Focus. On. Him.

Discernment

If you were to ask anyone who knows me where my favorite place on Earth is, they will tell you the lake. With close family having a lake home, I have spent my entire life enjoying the lake life. And I freaking love it like mad.

One of my favorite things I love about lake life is the early mornings. When the sun is coming up on the horizon, when the birds and bugs start singing, and when the water is like glass. It brings a sense of peace to me that I can't find in most places. And it brings a promising feeling of a greater day and a greater life.

But as I'm enjoying my peaceful bliss, it's inevitable that at some point in the morning, that peace will be disrupted with a boat blazing through my peaceful sheet of glass, leaving ripple effects.

Have you ever been in the water when a big boat goes by? If so, you have probably experienced what it's like to go through an actual ripple effect.

First, big waves will thrash you around. Eventually, the waves get smaller, and although they might not knock you around, you will still feel them. Then, at some point, the waves will completely calm, and you are in stillness again. This process takes some time to go through.

After that, you likely won't even think about those ripple effects or the boat that caused them.

Until....

It happens again. And then again. And again. Until eventually, your body poops out, and you head to shore where you can recuperate.

This cycle mirrors the ripple effect of the adversity that we face in life. Paralysis will cause waves in our lives that will eventually exhaust us physically and mentally.

Without question though God promises us that in those times that cause ripples—the suffering, the grieving, the failures, the disappointments, the anxieties—we can turn to him. He will help us restore our peace and positive outlook in life.

God's ultimate desire for us is to *choose* to achieve peace and lead a positive life without repeatedly subjecting ourselves to ripple effects. He calls us to have discernment.

It may be a relationship, a job, or an addiction causing the ripple effect in your life. It could be a habit, behavior, or wound. The list could go on and on. Regardless of what it is, our bodies, physically and mentally, cannot endure being tossed around forever. Eventually, we will wear out. It's at that point we have the choice to make that change in life or drown.

One of my favorite stories in the Bible came after the feeding of 5,000 when Jesus instructed his disciples to go ahead of him and cross to the other side of the lake. After managing all the people that remained, Jesus headed to the hills to pray. It was in the middle of the night when the disciples ran into some trouble. Weather had come on, and they were fighting heavy waves. They were terrified.

That's when they saw someone walking on water toward them. They were terrified at first, thinking it was a ghost. Jesus encouraged them,

"Take courage! It is I. Don't be afraid."
Matthew 14:27

But it was then that Peter called out to Jesus:

*"Lord, if it's really you, tell me to come to you,
walking on water."*
Matthew 14:28

So, Jesus did. He told Peter to come.

And this is what I love about the story. Peter just launched. This crazy guy jumped from a boat in a raging storm to get to Jesus. And as a result, Jesus rewarded him with a miracle. Peter walked on water.

Nothing was holding Peter back from trusting that Jesus would care for him. Nothing was holding him back from blindly trusting Jesus' power. He didn't need anything other than Jesus to be comfortable making the impossible happen.

Imagine the impact that Peter's faith had on his discernment. By all accounts, what Jesus was telling him to do was impossible, right?

But Peter's discernment, to consider things in the same way that Jesus does, changed everything for him. It changed his normal view of what was possible in the world.

This same impact that Jesus had on Peter is what he wants for us too. He wants us to see things through his eyes. He wants us to keep our eyes on him in all that we do. Then it's his wisdom that is helping us discern, not the influences of the outside world.

What does that mean for you when it comes to the paralysis in your life? It means that we need to arm ourselves with the wisdom of God to help us discern in our lives. We need to spend time with him, pray to him, and bury ourselves in the Bible so we can surround ourselves with the wisdom of his word.

Most importantly, we need to not take our eyes off him. That's how we will stay afloat. Peter learned the hard way: as he was walking on water and the waves started coming at him, he was terrified and began to sink.

Peter took his focus off Jesus, and all went to hell in a handbasket. Can you relate to this? When you focus on the fear instead of the faith, do you too start to sink?

The greatest news in the story came next.

> *"Save me, Lord!" he shouted. Jesus immediately reached out and grabbed him.*
>
> ### *Matthew 14:30–31*

This story is so especially important for us to relate to. God gives us discernment about what to do about the paralysis in our lives. Whether we are caught up in ripple effects or giant waves, he wants us to make the choice to keep our focus on him and swim to safety. He doesn't want us to stay there in fear, drowning.

But Jesus also proved how merciful he is. When we try to follow him and fail, he will rescue us. If our fear becomes greater than our faith and we start going under, he will reach out and grab us. It's just up to us to discern whether we should take his hand.

Because of all of this, we can't be afraid to jump. If Peter can walk on water, then imagine what God can do for us. If God tells you to do it, do it. He will help you. We can't be afraid of doing the crazy.

Doing

When I set out to be a small business owner in 2016, I. Could. Not. Wait. Oh, my gosh, I could not wait. I had more than my fill of corporate hoopla. The forecasts. The revisions. The micromanagement. BLEH! I was more than over it.

I could not wait to be my own boss.

The freedom from structure, from politics, from the pressure! Pure bliss is all that I imagined in my head. Aaaah. My life was about to change in two shakes. I was going to be my own boss.

That was four years ago. My, how time changed things. It didn't really turn out like I expected it to be.

I became my own worst boss . . . and my worst employee.

I don't want to confuse you too much to start, so I should clarify. I did build a successful business that has been going strong. I did accomplish *most* of what I set out to do—work less, mom more, make as much money. These things I did.

But I was behind in the most important thing I set out to do. I started my own business so I could work part-time to the tune of twenty hours per week. That would free me up to use the rest of my time to build a women's ministry.

That was not what ended up happening. I wasn't giving enough time to God.

I shouldn't be too hard on myself, I do realize. The decision I made was to chase two dreams at once: be a consultant and start a ministry. Both of these required lot of brain space. And strategy. And action. And I did make some progress.

But where I failed was trying to be a boss of two different locations *and* the employee at two different locations. Oy vey!

It had been so demanding! Amanda the business boss wanted Amanda the business employee to be working on the strategy for business, but Amanda the business employee was dreaming about the ministry and, subsequently, procrastinating on the business.

Then the next day, Amanda the ministry employee would be stressed about the lack of work that was done by Amanda the business employee, and nothing would get done. Amanda the business boss would then subsequently worry and procrastinate.

All the while, Amanda the ministry boss was feeling the stress of Amanda the ministry employee not showing up for work and instead would chase Amanda the business employee's squirrels. More procrastination.

And to top it all off, when Amanda the ministry employee finally showed up for work, she could not stay on task with the plan that Amanda the ministry boss laid out for her. She chased more squirrels, thus ministry procrastination.

Typing that made me stressed!

The vicious cycle continued.

That is until "Get your crap together, woman" happened.

Or kind of. God wouldn't really speak that way. But it was ultimately the message he was trying to portray in my prayer time with him.

"Get your crap together, woman" is exactly what I needed to do. I needed to get better at time management and prioritization. And I needed to do less of squirrel chasing and procrastination.

And so, I would hear that and respond by trying to be my own better boss, only to find the same result. Over and over again. I found myself obsessing over being in control, only to find both missions spiraling out of control, and my big dreams somehow kept getting further and further away. More and more procrastination.

Until I fired myself as boss. Gave myself the ol' pink slip from both jobs. Sent my own boss-self packing. I told myself, "You're fired!"

Surprised then that you are reading this book? Surprised that I somehow made it? Surprised that I somehow finished one of the umpteen million projects? Yeah, me too.

But, to your benefit, I'm going to let you in on the secret.

I hired a new boss. And you want to know who it was?

God. That's who. God the Almighty is now the boss man at RightHand LLC and AmandaMotivates Ministry. He's in the corner window office, and I'm in the cube. He's got the front space parking spot, and I'm in the back lot.

The best thing is he didn't cost me a thing. Other than maybe my ego.

One of the most difficult struggles we have with focusing is getting out of our own way to make room for God to lead the way. It is so hard. Especially when we can't see all the specific places in our life he wants to lead us to.

One area of our lives that we so often overlook as being paralyzing is the workplace. The failures and frustrations we feel, the demanding expectations we have for and from others—the workplace list of paralysis is mighty!

The workplace also happens to be one of the hardest places for us to turn over anything to God. Especially our paralysis.

We are the experts, after all, right? We are the only ones who can do our jobs, right? We are the only ones with good ideas, right? More often than not, we go about our workdays grappling with office politics and task lists and duties without even turning to God to help guide us along the way.

When people say, "Work sucks," this is why! It's often one of the most paralyzing existences in our lives. And to top it off, the stress and anxiety that workplace paralysis creates is often the fuse that lights the rest of the paralyzing areas of our lives. We take it home with us, and it turns into more unhealthy burdens.

Too often, the place where we are "doing" a good majority of our life is where we aren't "doing" our walk with God. And it's where we perhaps need to the most.

I first introduced God into my corporate work life in more of an "HR" way first. I first started asking him to take over when I needed to have difficult conversations or when I didn't know how to handle someone. I once had an employee who just could not see eye to eye with me, and it didn't matter what I did to try to smooth out our relationship on my own.

But when I turned it over to God, it became easier for me to manage. I remember praying to God before meeting with him and literally saying, "Jesus take the wheel." Doing so would always lead to a more productive conversation. While it didn't work out in the end, I'm confident that with God by my side, I did my part.

But inviting God to be my boss meant something entirely different. It meant giving up full control of not just my business and ministry but my day-to-day activities. I put him in charge of telling me what to do every single day.

How do I do that? I pray in the morning and ask him, "God, what's your plan for me today?" And I write down what's placed on my heart. It's as simple as that. God the boss lays out the plan.

I can't underscore enough what hiring God the boss has done for the "doing" part of my business and the ministry. The first day he was on the job, I wrote an entire chapter in a book. The next day, I tackled all my consultancy tasks, wrote some more, had a few coaching calls, and had time to enjoy a sauna, wine, and some Netflix. He literally quadrupled my productivity, if not more.

To top it all off, he taught me how patience can actually lead to abundance sooner. I was feeling so frustrated because I felt like I was running the race so hard but I was always falling behind. God taught me that at his pace, I can outperform myself in any race I've ever run. Even if I'm running slower! This has been the ultimate game changer.

Going to God every day has slowed me down but sped up the progress in my life. It's sped up my spiritual connection with him. It's sped up my growth and maturity as a child of God. And it has sped up my work in my business and my mission.

Sometimes in life, we can feel like we are "doing" a lot of "doing." But if we aren't getting the things done that we need to, which includes making the changes that God wants us to make, then that "doing" isn't leading to what God wants to be done.

Instead, when we go to God and ask him what he wants to be done and how he wants us to do it, we can honestly end up feeling like we are "doing" a lot less but getting more stuff done.

Bottom line: I can one hundred percent tell you that my business me and ministry me are more successful because I fired boss me. And I'm a better me. Perhaps the best me I've ever been.

This is the result we can expect when we focus on God. And, when we get out of his way and make the space for him to lead us in *everything* we do.

The next time you are frustrated at work, ask God to lead you through it. The next time you are pondering the next big job decision, ask God to make it for you. And the next time you are dreaming a big dream, ask God to be your boss and make it happen. God the boss will not disappoint.

It's time for the paralysis in your life to change. The next time you want to distract yourself with social media, ask God to show you instead where you should spend your time. The next time you are trembling with the fear of the big change, ask God to show you instead what would provide you peace. The next time you feel guilty about a temporary fail, ask God how to step around it.

When we focus on "doing" life with God, our daily "doing" will look different. Our progress will speed up. And the results we are desiring in our hearts and minds will happen.

Rehabilitation Questions

When we refocus our focus on God's ability to help us overcome our paralysis, we can find victory. Take some time to reflect on these questions.

1. Distractions

What distractions are happening in your life that are keeping you from focusing on overcoming your paralysis? What distractions are keeping you from turning to God to help you focus on finding freedom? Is technology or something else stealing the time you have to invest in finding peace? What can you do to limit those distractions and find more time with God?

2. Discernment

How does the story of Peter choosing to trust Jesus resonate with you? How does it make you feel about choosing to trust Jesus in the difficult circumstances in your life? How can you use Jesus to help you use discernment when navigating the paralyzing areas of your life?

3. Doing

When it comes to the things you are doing daily in life, how much are you engaging Jesus? How often do you find yourself turning over to God the difficult decisions that come up during the course of your day? Ponder what it could do for you to go to God daily and ask him what he wants you to accomplish and navigate for the day.

Comfortable with Uncomfortable

"Father, if you are willing, please take this cup of suffering away from me. Yet I want your will to be done, not mine."

Luke 22:41–42

Recently, I learned I was going to have to get uncomfortable for a while. Like super uncomfortable. Like running around naked uncomfortable. Almost.

I learned from my dermatologist that I needed to lay off wearing makeup for a while due to a skin issue that needed to heal.

Seriously, girls, this was a horrible reality for me. Beyond uncomfortable. This bare-naked face is not for the world to see. I have rosacea, wrinkles, paleness, and disappearing eyeballs. My eyes just disappear into my face without the mascara. I'm scary ugly without my makeup disguise. It's a wonder my husband will even sleep beside me.

I was so uncomfortable with this situation that I had been plotting how to go about my life without my face on. What covert operations can I implement to tackle my grocery shopping without anyone noticing? How do I convince the bank to give me my cash without revealing my identity? How do I renew my driver's license without taking a picture? Help!

You see, I couldn't let anyone see the real me. Nopety nope. That's too uncomfortable. At least for the time being.

The one saving grace I had was that I knew if I endured this suffering of naked face, I would get back to a face that I was not ashamed of, that did not feel ugly, that would feel right again.

I just had to be comfortable with being uncomfortable for the time being. I had to be reassured that that disruption in my life was for the better, and confident in knowing that that uncomfortable transition was only temporary.

In the entire history of time, there has never been anything comfortable about change. It's almost like we humans reject it like a donated organ. We recognize change as a foreign body, and even though we know that it's what we need and will make us better in the long run, our instinct is to say, "No, thank you."

This is the reality when we decide to make changes with the things that paralyze us. When we get to the point of knowing that we need to make that big change in our lives, we reject it, despite knowing that the change is exactly what we need to make our lives better.

The saving grace we have is that God will help us through that suffering of change. He will help us deal with shame. He will help us through the ugliness of the battle. And he will help us to find the beauty in our lives again.

We just have to be comfortable with being uncomfortable for a time. We have to be reassured that this disruption in our lives is for the better, and confident in knowing that this uncomfortable transition is only temporary.

Take David, for example. There couldn't have been anything comfortable about sleeping in caves in the wilderness as he was running from his enemies. I mean, imagine it. Sleeping on rocks with bugs and snakes. Even thinking about it makes me uncomfortable. Then top that off with the fear of someone always trying to cut his head off. Not a comfortable life to live!

But the one thing we are certain about with David is that despite how uncomfortable his circumstances were, he was comfortable with God's ability to rescue him from it. He never stopped having faith in him.

Later in life, David had to get comfortable with even more uncomfortable times. I've discussed David's horrible acts. It seems to me that he sinned like that because he was on a power trip. So, imagine how uncomfortable it had to be for him to surrender all that ego to God, to hand over that power. It couldn't have been easy.

I have to imagine, even though it was highly likely that David was very uncomfortable having to humble himself, he was, in fact, completely *comfortable* with knowing that God would bless him for surrendering.

Just as David did, we too need to get comfortable with uncomfortable. We need to start making the uncomfortable adjustments in our lives while taking comfort in the good work that God plans to do.

As you move forward, it will help to recognize how to get comfortable by navigating the following uncomfortable stages:

1. The Transition
2. The Change
3. The Grief
4. The Resistance

The Transition

I live in the Midwest. We don't have oceans, but we have seasons. All four of them. It is such a gift to experience the prime of our seasons. Every one of them is so beautiful. Even the winter. I mean, who doesn't like a white Christmas, right?

But with seasons comes the change of seasons. And there is one change of season that is always a tough one to endure: the end of winter. It starts with enduring ridiculously frigid temperatures for a few months. And I'm talking temperatures so cold that when it gets to thirty degrees, we are running around in our bikinis because it's sixty degrees warmer than it had been for four weeks prior. Ridiculous.

Then the sun starts baking and melting all of the snow. You'd think this would be a joyous occasion. But it's not. What's left underneath is this soggy, ugly, depressing mess. The grass shows no signs of becoming green again and looks as though life has been choked out of it. The brown of dead foliage just sucks, so far in contrast to the bright colors it radiated just a season back. And lest we forget the endless piles of wet, smelly dog poop that defrost from the frozen tundra. The transition from winter to spring is yucky. It's often a depressing time for many.

But what we cannot see under the depressing mess is the new life forming underneath it. There are good things just around the corner. The trees will bud, the grass will change, and the plants will begin to sprout. There is so much to look forward to just around the corner of this transition.

But where do our human instincts tend to focus? We don't focus on that hopeful future. Instead, we wallow in the midst of our darkest days.

Silly us. We should not have such despair. We know what is around the corner. Spring has never not come. Never! New life *always* arrives.

Imagine the anticipation, excitement, and hope we would feel if we would look past the dead in front of us and picture the life blooming underneath.

The same goes for our lives with Jesus. When we are going through the darkest of days, we struggle to look beyond the dark. We find ways to stay in that state and wallow in it. We find comfort in being Mrs. Poopy Pants.

Instead, imagine if we were to view those darkest days as a transition. If we were able to look beyond the darkness in our lives and at the new life that God is creating for us around the corner. If we were able to be comfortable with uncomfortable.

Without a doubt, this is how Jesus navigated his days on Earth. Imagine how uncomfortable he must have felt leading up to his crucifixion. In fact, in the days leading up to his arrest, Jesus sweat drops of blood. That had to be uncomfortable. This discomfort was demonstrated when Jesus said to his disciples,

"My soul is crushed with grief to the point of death."

Matthew 26:38

But then he demonstrated how he got comfortable with the discomfort he was in.

He went on a little farther and bowed with his face to the ground, praying, "My Father! If it is possible, let this cup of suffering be taken away from me. Yet I want your will to be done, not mine."

Matthew 26:39

Jesus then demonstrated his comfort in God's will.

> *Then Jesus left them a second time and prayed, "My*
> *Father! If this cup cannot be taken away unless I drink it,*
> *your will be done."*

Matthew 26:42

It was then that an extremely painful battle started. Jesus was brutally scourged. A painful crown of thorns was placed upon his head. Although he was weak from the torture, he was made to carry the very heavy burden of the cross. His shoulders were dislocated. He was nailed to the cross through his hands and his feet and then made to suffer an excruciating death on the cross.

Jesus was more uncomfortable than any of us could ever imagine.

How do you think Jesus got through all of this?

Because Jesus was comfortable with accepting God's will. He was comfortable with what he saw beyond pain. He knew how much the pain was worth. He knew it was for us to have eternal life in heaven with God the Father.

He knew he wasn't going to heaven alone. He was taking his children with him. Through his painful crucifixion, he was leaving this world behind and taking the sins of his children with him so they could one day join him in heaven. Jesus was not focusing on his uncomfortable pain in his final hours. He was focusing on the comfort that God the Father would bring him and us for eternity.

Wow, just wow.

Imagine if you endured your pain and suffering in the same way. If you accepted God's will and the discomfort it sometimes comes with. If you saw beyond the pain and instead viewed it as just a transition.

Would it change things for you to take the focus off your discomfort and instead focus on the comfort of eternal life with God the Father?

*Because of the joy awaiting him, he endured the cross,
disregarding its shame. Now he is seated in the place of
honor beside God's throne.*

Hebrews 12:2

It's amazing what God can do with our darkness. Just like God took the darkness of Jesus' suffering and turned it into the beautiful light that provides hope in our lives, we too can have our darkness turned into light. Our paralysis doesn't have to stay doomy and gloomy. He can make something amazing and beautiful bloom from it. Think about this amazing hope. The old will fall away, and you will be made new.

To take advantage of this offer from God, we have to look at things differently. We have to look beyond what we see to the world we can't see. The one that God sees.

What God sees in that uncomfortable transition from paralysis to purpose is full of life! It's full of hope and peace. It's full of comfort.

When you navigate this transition differently, your prospect for making the change in your life will look different too.

The Change

Perhaps no story speaks to me as much as the woman at the well. In John 4, Jesus came across a Samaritan woman at the well. This Samaritan woman had some definite baggage. She was known for getting around. And back in the day, she would have to draw water in the middle of the day because it was not appropriate for others to be seen with her drawing water in the morning and evening. Especially a Jew and a man.

Despite this, Jesus went to ask her to draw water for him. During their encounter, Jesus essentially told her everything about her life. They had never met, and here he was spilling out her life story upon her. Miraculous. Obviously, that alone was a life-changing moment for her. But then he drops a truth bomb. He tells her that he is the Messiah.

What happened next is where I relate to her. This broken, shamed girl runs back to town to tell everyone about Jesus. Literally left her job of drawing water to witness about Jesus Christ.

Think about the gravity of this moment. There couldn't have been anything comfortable about this for the Samaritan woman. Who would give her credibility given her background? Who would even care to listen? Who would believe such a crazy story? Despite all of this, she got comfortable with doing the uncomfortable for the sake of Jesus.

Jesus knew he could use her. Broken woman and all. He knew she would step in faith. He knew her witness would draw people near. And he knew that believers would follow.

And they did. John 4:41 NIV says, "many more became believers."

> *They said to the woman, "We no longer believe just because of what you said; now we have heard for ourselves, and we know that this man really is the Savior of the world."*
>
> ### *John 4:42 NIV*

When I left my career aspirations behind to follow God and become a witness for him, I'm certain my feelings were the same as the Samaritan woman's: super excited, totally terrified, and a wee bit crazy. I can only imagine her thought process as she was running back into the town. A battle between who she'd been and the transformation that Jesus had just given her.

I too had this mind battle. One of the hardest things about being on my journey of change was the split personality I've felt. If I'm being honest with you, it's felt a bit Jekyll and Hyde for me. There's the person that I've been and the person that God's been shaping me to be, and sometimes those two sides don't align.

There's the side of me that loves God and will follow him blindly as his faithful servant. Then there's College Amanda who has not necessarily grown up yet. I still like toilet humor, drink beer, and as my good friend says, "I love Jesus, but I swear a little."

Don't get me wrong. There's plenty of things I've left in my college days. And that's a good thing. But there are some things I just haven't grown out of. And can't seem to. They are the things that I just keep taking with me to the well.

But Jesus keeps meeting me there. Regardless, he keeps showing up and revealing himself to me. Over and over again. He's not giving up on me as a witness. He's been relentless.

The challenge I've felt is despite this change and transformation that God has been making in my life, I have receiver's guilt. I imagine the Samaritan woman probably felt a little bit like this. I've felt unworthy of this transformation. I've felt unqualified for being his witness. I've felt like God got it all wrong picking me.

Why do I feel this way? It's not because of my own faith. Not at all. I feel rock solid in my faith. I feel I could conquer the world with it.

I feel this way because I'm afraid of how I am perceived by others. I'm insecure. I'm worried that the two skins I'm wearing are confusing them. I'm worried they view me as a hypocrite.

How can I possibly love God so much to blindly follow him down a path of ministry and then be found drinking a frothy cold one telling an all too colorful story?

These are the worries that consume me!

But this is where God stops me. And he stops you too. If you too are battling the old you and the new you, God says stop. He knows that this change can be hard. He knows it's not going to happen overnight. And he knows who you are.

God does not want to deny who we are. Rest assured in that. He created you knowing full well who you are. Those things in your life that you are insecure about, he will use.

I mean, look at the Samaritan woman. Look at how he used her. Jesus could have met anyone at the well and demonstrated his powers and inspired someone else to drop everything and run to town to tell all the others. But he didn't.

He. Used. Her.

He used her brokenness. He used her faith. He used her witness.

In the same way, he's using me right now. He's using the very things that I feel insecure about to reach you right now.

It doesn't take a perfect, Christian-living woman to minister to people. It just takes a person willing to step outside their comfort zone and get uncomfortable pursuing God's mission for them.

This is his plan for you too. You are the woman at the well. He wants to reveal his powers to you. He wants you to make uncomfortable changes in your life that he can use. He wants you to witness. We aren't called to disguise our fundamental failings; we are called to use them.

And God knows that these changes can be hard. That's how our spiritual growth happens. When we navigate these big changes in our lives. This is when we begin to wear the new skin.

When we get comfortable with uncomfortable, it means that we can accept who we are and who we've been without denying who it is that he wants us to be.

The Grief

Recently, I've had some people in my life dealing with significant amounts of grief. Grief over lost relationships, lost opportunities, and lost life.

Everyone's grief has been paralyzing for them. It's been impossible for them to see beyond the pain, impossible for them to see hope for the future, and impossible for them to leave the past behind.

And while all of them are experiencing grief for various reasons, there is one common thread to their grief: imagining a life of living without.

When we begin the transformation of living a life without our paralysis, we too will experience the same kind of grief. We too will struggle with imagining a life of living without.

Here's why.

As we change our lives to live a life without the things that paralyze us, we take on a new life. We shed our old skin to wear our new one.

When you do this, you can experience grief over the loss of the old you. You are saying goodbye to someone you know very well. And even though that someone (you) may have caused you a lot of pain and agony over the years, you were attached.

I've been experiencing a lot of grief on this ministry journey. No doubt that God has transformed my heart in a big way. And sometimes, that transformation in my heart doesn't match the person that I've always been.

I think most would say that I have enjoyed trying to be the life of the party for my entire life. Not gonna lie. Some of my best comedic performances have been when I've been well served. I always enjoyed being College Amanda. I've always been. Mrs. Party Pants.

What's played out with my heart transformation is that I've recognized the need to tone it down. Don't get me wrong, God's not telling me to not be fun, but my heart has certainly recognized that if I'm going to try to bring people to Jesus, I need to start acting a little more like him. And Jesus, while he drank wine, I'm guessing he was not one to down a whole bottle, drop some swears, and moon people. Not him.

I have grieved over recognizing the need to say goodbye to the old me. Even grieved over saying goodbye to living the life where I just didn't care what people thought of me. It seemed easier in some sense. But at the same time, I wonder, "Will people even like the new me over the old me?"

Despite that grief though, I'm growing comfortable with the new simmered-down me. Still fun but more self-controlled. Still me but sprinkled with more of that Fruit of the Spirit. It's definitely a continuous work in progress finding that balance. I'm working on it, of course.

Because that's what happens when we draw closer to him—sanctification. The more we draw closer to him, the more we become like him.

And what I know beyond a doubt is that the new me is better. She just is. She doesn't make me cringe as much. She doesn't make me regret as much. She doesn't make me shake my head as much.

You will find this too as you navigate the grief of the old you when you begin to shape into the new you. Be comfortable in knowing that the shedding of the old you will result in you being made new. Even if people don't recognize you, in the end, you will feel so much better. Be comfortable with that uncomfortable stage of grief, knowing that the new you will be someone you like much better.

The Resistance

Sometimes, people become so uncomfortable with the transformation and the grief that comes with it that we begin to become resistant to it. We dig our stubborn heels into the dirt and say, "Enough! I quit."

In other words, we choose to stay in our paralysis.

When we become too afraid of getting uncomfortable, oftentimes God will use some situation to make us uncomfortable with the things that are paralyzing us in our lives.

He doesn't want us to continue with those patterns and carry those burdens. He doesn't want us stuck and not progressing toward our purpose. It's imperative to him that we move forward.

So, at some stage of this resistance, God's going to use something in our paralyzed lives to make us super uncomfortable.

When I say that, I don't mean he will cause something bad to happen in our lives. But he will use circumstances in our paralysis to inspire us to make a change.

He will do so to get us to seek him. He will do this to get us to move to him. He will do this to help us find comfort in him.

This is what God did to David after he stole Bathsheba from Uriah and subsequently killed him. God made David uncomfortable. In fact, the Lord sent Nathan the prophet to have words with David. Specifically calling him out and threatening him:

> *"This is what the Lord says: Because of what you have done,*
> *I will cause your own household to rebel against you."*
>
> ### *2 Samuel 12:11*

God was done! He had given everything to David, including the entire kingdom of Israel. He had blessed him beyond measure. Clearly, David's power had gotten to his head, and he resisted God's desire to transform his heart. So, God intervened.

What followed was exactly what God had the prophet Nathan tell David was going to happen. His life went to crap, including his very own son decided that he wanted his dad dead. David's life became super uncomfortable.

The key to this story though is how David responded. He knew that he had resisted God and been disobedient. So, he repented. He recognized the discomfort, and it made him have a transformation in his heart. He didn't stay stuck in that crappy place. He turned to God for comfort throughout it all.

I experienced the resistance discomfort phase not too long ago. At the time, God was leading me to start this ministry, and I was paralyzed. I was working more than full-time in a job that I knew, in my heart, I did not want to do. I was managing the blending of five teenagers and had debt up the wazoo. So, when God laid on my heart to start this ministry, it just seemed more than I could manage.

I was working so hard to make time for the ministry. Usually, around 9 p.m., when the rest of my life had settled in for the day, I would start working on it. I was seriously burning the candles at both ends. And just when I thought I couldn't manage any more, God laid a doozy on me.

God: "My child, I want four hours a day."

Me: "Say what?"

I was already drowning! How could I possibly come up with four hours a day for God? I tried and tried for months, doing my absolute best to put in what I could, but I couldn't pull it off.

I knew in my heart that I needed to find a way. But I didn't do it. I was paralyzed by the worldly expectations I had for myself. I couldn't quit my job to start a ministry. That would be irresponsible, right? I was not comfortable with getting uncomfortable.

But I also knew I was resisting. I remember telling my husband, "God keeps poking me about this, and someday, he is just going to shove me in the back."

And he did.

Right before Christmas in 2016, the company I was working for was closing its doors. I was, for the first time in my life, without a job.

You would have thought that I would have been super uncomfortable with that situation. But believe it or not, I was not. I was excited. I was celebrating. I was comfortable. Because I knew that God was going to provide.

And he did.

I started my own consulting business that month. Within a few months, I landed a contract that would replace my income and require me to work only twenty hours per week. That's right. Do the math. That left me with twenty hours a week. Yep . . . four hours a day.

Pretty cool, huh?

Those times in our lives when God intervenes aren't always easy. But we can, ironically, find comfort when we are uncomfortable. We can be confident that when he is at work, great things are around the corner. We don't need to resist it. We need to take comfort in it.

The Importance

I recall a time when I was on my way back to the hospital to be with Todd, who was still in bed paralyzed. Despite being in the midst of one of my greatest life struggles, I had the windows down and belted some Christian praise. I was so hopeful and confident in what God was about to do. Although it was an uncomfortable time, I was comfortable being in it.

Then a song called "Love Come to Life" played on the radio by Big Daddy Weave. The lyrics talked about bringing love to life inside of us for the sake of showing the hopeless and broken world that God loves them. And it literally talked about breaking my heart until moving hands and feet. Seriously. Moving hands and feet! So relevant.

This song made my heart erupt. It had such meaning for that time and place in my life. I mean, c'mon, a song about moving hands and feet as we were battling my husband's paralysis just about blew me out of my seat.

This song spoke to the broken yet very hopeful place we were in our lives. His love was so alive in us then.

Well, God sure used the love that he was bringing to life inside us. No matter how uncomfortable God makes us, there is importance in it. He intends to use it.

We had a CaringBridge page to communicate with people how things were playing out with Todd. What poured into that journal was faith, hope, and love. There was not despair. There wasn't wallowing in tragedy. There was just his love coming to life.

Because of the spiritual transformation that God had already done in my heart before this difficult journey, I was comfortable being uncomfortable. And he used that.

We didn't realize at the time just how many people were following his journey. It turned out there were close to ten thousand page visits. Even people that we didn't know were following his progress. Thousands of people got to witness our faith in progress. First the blind faith:

> *Day 2: I won't stop telling him what I'm hearing from God in my prayers, and it's that he will be healed. It's been clearly revealed to me, and I'm going to make us hold onto that.*

Then the trust:

> *Day 4: Todd has been dealing with some major body shakes today. We think it's anxiety because it happens after he wakes up. I encouraged him to say a prayer for peace in the middle of a freaky set of shakes, so he did, and after a good thirty-second prayer, they stopped. And then he fell asleep. I think that was a good trusting-God moment for Todd.*

Then the miracle that followed:

> *Day 4, 1 hour later: Well apparently, my request for getting some good progress tomorrow was acted upon*

early. Tonight, we had awesome movement with that right leg. He lifted it off the bed a bit, pulled up with a bended knee some, and the big one . . . he pushed on my hand so hard with his leg that I couldn't keep him from straightening it. This was truly amazing and exciting for all of us to see.

It would be just a few days later that our CaringBridge world would see him take his first steps. And then, just a few days after that, they would see him cruising down the hallway with a walker, dancing a little jig. They got to witness God's miracle, and the promise kept that "He will be healed."

I can't be certain, but I sure hope that we reached those that don't know that God loves them, just as Big Daddy Weave wished. But I have to imagine that out of the many we reached, there were plenty who were moved by our faithful journey. We were bombarded with comments on how impressed people were by our faith and hope: *"God's promises and his glory are being revealed through you, Todd."*

I know that when I look back, I would never want Todd to go through what he had to go through again. But I'm not sure that I don't want to through what I went through again.

Does that sound totally crazy to you?

Don't get me wrong, it was an incredibly trying time. But it was also a profound spiritual experience. I would do it all over just to feel that incredible presence again. To hear his faithful promises and to see him deliver on them. To witness a miracle!

I'm not sure my heart has ever been fuller than it was during that tragedy. And I'm certain I have never loved more.

And what I can't argue with is that it happened for a reason. God fully intended for it to be used to reach people. Our comfortable experience with our uncomfortable situation hopefully will provide comfort to someone who has to be uncomfortable too.

Day 10: The reason I am sharing this story is because we truly believe that God had his hand in this, or should I say God had his hand in [Todd's]. The Bible talks a lot about patience and God working in his own time (Psalm 27:14, Galatians 6:9). Sometimes that timing isn't always as soon as we want, but the timing is always what is right. Today God's timing was perfect. And I believe it was perfect because he wanted us to be witnesses and share his incredible workings.

Your struggle with paralysis can have the same impact. He's ready for you to get comfortable with the uncomfortable part of changing. You don't have to wait for tragedy to strike. He's ready to work on what's already struck us. The painful paralysis that we are living day in day out, he's ready to heal. He is ready to rock your faith and hope. He's waiting for you to turn to him and to give it to him so he can do his mighty work and give you the miracle you need in your life.

And he's ready for you to be his witness about it all.

Rehabilitation Questions

It's always been said that change is uncomfortable. And it is true. But when we know that the change is for good, we know we need to be comfortable with the uncomfortable for the time being—and God can help us through that. Take some time to reflect on the following questions.

1. Transitions and Change

How do you handle transitions in your life when you know that you aren't navigating them alone? Does your attitude towards change happen when you consider that it may be God's will? How does it make you feel when you consider that your difficult transition from paralysis could be used in a good way? What verses can you discover that may help you navigate challenging times of change?

2. Grief

Have you ever felt the need to let a part of yourself go? Have you struggled with saying goodbye to the old you? At the same time, do you feel better about the new you? How can you lean into God to help you go through the stage of grieving over the life you previously led?

3. Resistance

Have you ever resisted making changes in your life that you knew you needed to make? How did that work out for you? Have you ever been hit with a big life correction that knocked you off your feet? Looking back, how would you handle that now given what you know? With what you are currently facing, what can you give to God that you haven't, to avoid being resistant to his will?

WHAT GOD WANTS FOR OUR
RECOVERY

Jesus Frees Us

For you have been called to live in freedom
my brothers and sisters.

Galatians 5:13

I recently watched a video of babies getting glasses for the first time. The cutest, most heartwarming videos ever, I swear. Each video shows a mama putting the glasses on the baby, and then the most remarkable reaction occurs: nearly every baby just freezes. They don't yank the foreign object off their faces or start to fuss over the discomfort. They just freeze and start to take all the sights in.

You can just see the amazement in their eyes. This world that was such a blur to them before suddenly clear as day. In every single case, when their parent speaks to them in their loving tone, their face lights up like the Eiffel Tower. The biggest, most beautiful baby smiles happen. The joy from these babies cannot be contained. They see a whole new world in front of them, and they are overjoyed.

I know many of you can relate with me when I say that this is what it's like when we see the hope that Jesus has for us in our lives—when he helps us see a beautiful light-filled world beyond the blurry, paralyzed lives that we are living.

The metaphor of Jesus being "the light of the world" is really simple. I mean, think about it. When light shines on things, they become more beautiful. When that sun comes out, everything becomes brighter. More vivid. More truth about each thing comes out. Colors. Details. Features.

Light is imperative in our lives. Without it, we simply would not have life. Nothing would grow. Energy would cease. Our bodies would starve.

We don't just need light. We love it. We crave it.

In contrast, can you think of a single thing that gains beauty in the darkness? I cannot. In fact, in darkness, beauty gets lost.

The same concept comes when we let God's light shine on us and through us. We become more beautiful, and we see things in a more beautiful light. It's like seeing a whole new world.

But we all have those moments when we follow darkness into a rabbit hole. Social media tends to do this to me. Reading negative, hateful posts can lead me down the same path. And as a result of following darkness, I can become darkness. Then ugliness comes out.

It's a shame when that happens because then people focus on the darkness in you. The light and beauty diminish in the eyes of those that we are supposed to be witnessing to.

We don't have to let darkness get its grip though. It can be controlled, especially when we give everything to Jesus.

I know it probably doesn't cross most people's minds to give their social media presence to Jesus, but imagine if it did. Imagine if social media was full of Jesus' light and that alone. Can you imagine that power? Can you imagine the amount of light that would shine?

As silly as that might sound, it's not. In fact, there isn't a single thing in our lives that we shouldn't give to Jesus. In everything we do, we are called to give it to him.

Jesus spoke about this when he was explaining to a group of followers about why he must die.

> *Jesus replied, "My light will shine for you just a little longer. Walk in the light while you can, so the darkness will not overtake you. Those who walk in the darkness cannot see where they are going. Put your trust in the light while there is still time; then you will become children of the light."*

> ### *John 12:35–36*

I shared previously what "walking" means in the Bible. It means *spiritual progress.* To walk in the light means we will make spiritual progress when we follow Jesus. A paralyzed life that follows Jesus will make progress to a life of freedom.

Jesus is our conduit to freedom. Plain and simple. Without following his light, our own selfish, sinful ways will continue to lead us to darkness. And as Jesus stated, in darkness, we can't see where the heck we are going!

Think about it. When we make crappy choices, can we see the dead-end road it leads to? Do we envision the pain in front of us? Do we focus on the trials we are about to endure?

No!

Of course, we don't. Because if we did, we wouldn't be heading down that road. Do you agree?

I mean, think about it. Do we put our hand on a hot burner on our stove? No! Because we are aware and can vividly imagine the pain that would be caused. We avoid it at all costs.

If we could see where our darkness was leading to, we would most certainly try to avoid it. But in darkness, we don't see it. We choose not to.

The only way to see where that darkness is leading to is through the light that Jesus shines for us. He lights our path. He helps us to see what's ahead. He helps us to steer ourselves back on course.

To overcome paralysis, we must walk. And walking in the light is our only option. Deciding to take a walk isn't one that God is going to make for us. It is one in which we will get to choose.

"Me Path" or "We Path"?

Jesus spoke to the people once more and said,
"I am the light of the world. If you follow me, you
won't have to walk in darkness, because you will
have the light that leads to life."

John 8:12

Choosing on our own to leave our lives of paralysis behind to live a life full of purpose will lead us down the path to freedom. This we can be confident in. This is what God wanted for us.

> *You were running the race so well. Who has held you*
> *back from following the truth? It certainly isn't God,*
> *for he is the one who called you to freedom.*

Galatians 5:7–8

One of the biggest choices we are given every day of our lives is the direction we are going to take. Which path are we going to choose? The choice is really simple. Do we walk in the light with God, the "we path"? Or do we walk alone in darkness, the "me path"?

I understand that with some things in life, we've survived walking on our own. Perhaps you're thinking, "Well, I've come this far, haven't I?" And rightly so; you likely have succeeded in areas of your life without God. Perhaps, you've also overcome some personal battles. I get that.

But at that point in our lives, when we are *paralyzed,* it means that the "me path" you have been on has failed. You are stuck. And you've been unable to move on your own.

There are two stages of paralysis we fall into in life.

The Unaware Stage

At this stage, we are unaware that we are even paralyzed. It begins when we start to lose control of our circumstances in some fashion. Then we start to feel anxious and fearful about those circumstances. At this stage, we haven't quite accepted that something needs to change.

The Aware Stage

This stage starts with the recognition of our paralysis. We recognize that we are stuck, and our circumstances need to change. Deep down inside, we want to do the right thing.

Then we come to the fork in the road.

This is the big decision. Which path are you going to take? The "me path" or the "we path" (you and God)?

One of these paths leads to more paralysis, and one of these leads to God's purpose. One path leads to the complacency of continued pain, and the other leads to a path of freedom.

The "Me Path"

This is the path we set out on without God. It typically plays out like this:

1. We realize something is wrong and consider changing our circumstances.
2. We become fearful and defiant of changing our circumstances.
3. We begin to have a hard time controlling our thoughts about our circumstances.
4. We might attempt to change those circumstances but fail.
5. We make excuses for failing.
6. Eventually, we no longer think doing the right thing is worth it.
7. This is when we hit the Complacent stage. We are paralyzed. Repeat and go back to the beginning.

Because paralysis is what keeps us from achieving God's purpose for our lives, this simply cannot be the path that we choose. Not if we are fully in this thing with God. To achieve that purpose, we must tap into God to remove the paralysis that keeps us from fulfilling that calling.

Which leads us to the "we path."

The "We Path"

The "we path" is all about setting out to overcome our paralysis with God by our side. This journey tends to play out like this:

1. We use God's word to find hope in changing our circumstances.
2. We develop trust in prayer with God that he can heal us.
3. We use God's power to help us move.
4. We use God's protection to help us overcome Satan's attacks.

5. We find peace in God's presence as he helps us move forward.
6. We give our bondage completely to God.
7. Then we hit the Freedom stage. We are released to fully pursue our purpose. We leave our former way of life and make progress.

Our choice. Choose the "me path," and you are choosing paralysis. Choose the "we path," and you are choosing freedom, purpose, and progress. This is the decision we are faced with. It's as simple as that. God lets us choose.

Your word is a lamp to guide my feet and a light for my path.

Psalm 119:105

The Path to Freedom

When we decide to take the "we path" over the "me path," it doesn't mean our decision-making is over. It's not like God just sets us on cruise control, and he carries us the rest of the way. We have a responsibility to continue to stay on that road. Unfortunately, our human nature will, almost inevitably, veer us off course at some point in time.

I don't know about you, but sometimes I feel like God chases me around trying to get me on the right path, and I run around pouncing on everything else. He jumps up and down, waving a red flag, hollering at me, "Get your crap together, woman," and I, as you know, chase squirrels.

As a result, there have been several moments where I've felt that I had no traction, no direction, and no progress . . . like I've been chasing my tail. And if I were to venture a guess, God feels like he's been herding a cat.

The Bible is clear about us being his sheep, and God, the shepherd, very much views us in that light. But sometimes, I have to imagine, God goes through periods where he feels he is actually herding cats.

Sheep are instinctively created to be herd and led. The sheep's flocking instinct allows sheepherders to look after and move large numbers of sheep. This is awesome for God because he obviously has a giant flock to lead and move to eternity. So, if they are instinctively following him, the job is easier.

But cats, on the other hand, are not instinctively created to be herd or led. Cats can't be controlled. Cats will do what they want. If I tried to get my cat to obey me, she would give me a snide scowl, give me a look that says, "bite me," then prance off. Cats, we can safely say, have a mind of their own. That's why so many people hate cats.

But here's the difference in my analogy between cats and people. We people are all instinctively created to be led by God. We are all created to be his sheep. But sometimes, we *choose* to act like cats instead.

- We refuse to listen.
- We refuse to obey.
- We choose to defy.
- We do our own thing.

And while that must frustrate the crap out of God, he loves us just the same.

Let's put this in perspective.

Our kids, for example. In their younger years, they follow us around constantly. Always at our heels, climbing into our beds, throwing a fit when we leave. They are created with the instinct to be led by us. They want us to be their shepherd.

But then . . . they become teenagers (for some, I realize this happens much sooner). They refuse to listen. They refuse to obey. They choose to defy. Despite how much we try to lead them in the right direction, they decide to do their own thing. They look at us with a snide scowl and whisper the words, "bite me" under their breath, then prance off.

This is so frustrating for us as parents! It's defeating. It's devastating. It may just be the hardest thing ever of all time. All that we have done to shape them, instantly destroyed. Having five teenagers in every grade of high school right now, I'm feeling this pain. Lord, help me!

Despite how well we've raised them, despite the values we've instilled in them, despite the great people they're created to be, there are points in kids' lives that they will do anything to avoid being controlled. They act like cats.

But that doesn't change how we feel about our children. Doesn't change the fact that we love them to our core. Doesn't change the fact that we want the very best life for them. And it doesn't change the fact that we will do anything in our power to help lead them again.

That's how God feels about us. Even though sometimes we look in God's direction and run the opposite way, he will always be trying to herd us. We don't have to be the easy sheep; we can be the crazy cat. He will always welcome us back to his flock. He will always welcome us back to the "we path."

God does not hate cats. In fact, God is a cat hoarder. He's got a boatload of 'em, and he's loving them to death.

Here's what God wants all of us cats to know. We are all on a mission. We are all following the same direction to the endpoint in our lives: freedom in eternity. How we get from where we are now, the "me path" or "we path," is up to us. Do we choose to be a sheep or a cat?

Do not be afraid, little flock, for your Father
has been pleased to give you the kingdom.

Luke 12:32 NIV

One thing our great shepherd knows for sure is if you are a sheep following right behind him on the "we path," it's sure to be a lot easier to get there. We can go with our instincts:

To follow him.

To let him guide us.

To be his disciple.

To let him direct our decisions.

If we choose to ignore those instincts and defy and we refuse to listen and obey, it's okay. While our journey might be tougher, we can always come back to him. We should always come back to him. He wants us to come back to him. He wants us to be the cat that can't stay away.

For this is what the Sovereign LORD says: I myself will search and find my sheep. I will be like a shepherd looking for his scattered flock. I will find my sheet and rescue them from all the places where they were scattered on that dark and cloudy day.

Ezekiel 34:11–12

My rebellious years have been pretty abundant in my life. For many years, I was paralyzed with codependency. And on multiple occasions, God tried to lead this crazy cat to freedom from it.

The challenge is codependency is really a control condition. And what happens is that in order to keep your life from spinning out of control, you start to control everything around you.

When you have a control issue and you go down the "me path," it's not the recipe for success. In fact, you end up creating a situation that spins you even more out of control. By the time you get to that Complacent stage, you've come up with so many excuses that you've actually convinced yourself things are okay. But they are not.

The control I was experiencing was paralyzing. I was in my own way. It led me to a place of hopelessness. I was stuck, and there was no way out of it.

Until I turned to God.

When I turned toward him and gave the "we path" a try and stayed on course, it changed everything. I had hope. I believed. I felt powerful. I trusted. I had steam.

I'm not going to lie to you though. It was a challenge to stay on course. Oh, man, was it. It was terrifying at times. I wanted more than anything to jump back over to the "me path" and take a bath in my complacency. While it was not the easier route in the long run, I was tempted by its short-term relief.

But I stayed the course. God came through with each difficult step. His strength in me persevered.

It was not a quick journey. But it got easier with time. The more I trusted and had faith, the more of his presence and power I felt and endured. After a while, the confidence in my ability to get through it increased. Eventually, I got to a place where I was able to fully give that codependency to God.

I found freedom. And every single part of that journey was worth it to get to this side.

When I was going through that journey several years ago, I blogged as a way to get through it. It was healing for me. I came across the following journal post recently:

> *The following is from my Rick Warren devotional this morning: "He comforts us when we are in trouble so that we can share that same comfort with others in trouble. We share in the terrible sufferings of Christ, but also in the wonderful comfort he gives." (2 Corinthians 1:4–5) Your greatest ministry will flow out of your pain—not out of your strengths or your talents but out of the painful experiences of your life. It is your weaknesses that help other people in their need, not your strengths."*

> *Throughout this nightmare I've been living, I've found healing in helping others. Whether it's been through sharing Scripture, helping a friend through their own trials, or writing this blog . . . I've found fulfillment in the hope that my pain can somehow help someone else end theirs. My brokenness is out there . . . I've laid it all out. And I'm not going to stop. I feel a calling to help others in my situation. Not sure exactly where God is leading me, but what I feel is bigger than this blog. Please say some prayers to have God shine that light for me and direct me down the path he has for me.*

It's crazy to look at my words from back then. I was in the midst of one of the most painful times in my life, but I knew that God would use it. I knew that it had a purpose. But I had no idea what it was. Nor did I consider it something big. Little did I know back then that God would lead me to this ministry and to something as big as writing a book.

You might be going through a similarly difficult journey right now. You might be enduring the most painful time in your life. You might be feeling terrified, hopeless, and lost. But there is freedom in front of you if you just turn to him. There is purpose in it.

God will use your pain. He will use your weakness. He will use it all to help others. To lead others to Christ. To help others find freedom.

Recovery Questions

It's always been said that change is uncomfortable. And it is true. But when we know that the change is for good, we know we need to be comfortable with the uncomfortable for the time being—and God can help us through that. Take some time to reflect on the following questions.

1. Spiritual Progress

When you think about the life that you are leading, would you say that you follow light or darkness? Do you portray light or darkness to those around you? Have you ever had a spiritual awakening where God's truth and light shine through that darkness? If not, what could you be doing to seek that?

2. "Me Path" or "We Path"

In the past, where have you typically found yourself navigating life's difficult journeys: on a path alone or with God? Where has that taken you and what did that journey look like? What path are you on right now? If you are on the "me path," what's it going to take to get you to jump to the other path with God?

3. Freedom

Do you feel that you are letting God lead you, or God is having to herd you? How much are you letting God guide you? How much control are you giving God to help you overcome your paralysis? Are you ready to get on the "we path" and let God lead you to freedom?

Repurpose Our Purpose

We know that all things work together for good to them who love God, to them who are the called according to his purpose.

Romans 8:28 KJV

So often in life, we only negatively view our struggles. I mean, duh, right? Why wouldn't we? Struggles suck!

But what happens when we view our struggles in a different light? In a positive light?

It can be done. Hear me out.

Most people know someone or have been someone who has served in the armed forces. I believe it would be rare to come across someone who has served that considered military training as nothing but a super happy, enjoyable experience. Perhaps there are a few exceptions to the rule, so please show me some grace for this perspective. The tales I've heard are that it's grueling, exhausting, painful, and an incredible mental battle. Despite this extremely challenging experience, they endure it because their minds are focused on their mission. When they come out the other side, they get to celebrate their strength, commitment, and an incredible accomplishment.

So, imagine your paralysis struggles in life in the same light. What if you were to view them as your basic training for the mission God has in your life—for the purpose that he has for you.

Would you view those struggles differently? Would you celebrate your ability to overcome them differently? Would you use it for good?

The truth is that our struggles are intended to be our training. To not only help us navigate our future struggles in a way that leans on him, but to also arm us with the wisdom we need to be on mission for him and to serve our godly purpose.

It does not matter if we have chosen a path of ministry in our lives at all. When we accept Jesus as our ultimate commander, we are all drafted to be his warrior. Every single one of us. We are all called to serve him in one way, shape, or form.

God will use our paralysis to shape us for the purpose that he has intended for us.

We can't continue training for the rest of our lives though. We have to eventually graduate from it and move on to the mission. When we continue living with paralysis in our lives and don't move beyond the training phase, it affects our progress to fulfilling God's purpose for us.

And as much as some of you may have a hard time believing it, we all have a godly purpose in our lives. Some of you may know what that is, some of you may think you know what it is, and some of you may have no clue. Either way, it's okay. But no matter what, we must recognize that it is there, and God is reliant on us to overcome the burdens that are keeping us from fulfilling it.

Through this chapter, we will begin to understand what God has revealed about our purpose and how we can use what God teaches us about removing the paralysis in our lives to fulfill it.

God's Fingerprint on Our Lives

Have you ever considered the incredible creation of the human body? It's hard to look at the human body and not think that God has a pretty creative imagination. I mean, think about it. From bones to tissues to cells to nerves and all the detailed inner workings within. Bodies are freaking weird, are they not? Think about all our guts and how they work. Totally bizarre. But also, totally amazing.

If this is what we can see, imagine what God can see!

God didn't make all of our bodies to look or be the same. We aren't a bunch of clones walking around. We are very uniquely and perfectly created to be who we are and what we are. Even the gaps in our teeth and our hairy moles.

> *For you formed my inward parts; you knitted me together in my mother's womb. I praise you, for I am fearfully and wonderfully made. Wonderful are your works; my soul knows it very well.*
>
> **Psalm 139:13–14 ESV**

We are wonderfully made by God himself. This is true for our bodies, our personalities, and our purpose in life.

Take, for example, fingerprints. Some amazingly smart, nerdy people at the National Forensic Science Technology Center discovered that "no two people have ever been found to have the same fingerprints—including identical twins." No two people. There are gazillions of people on this planet . . . and no one shares the same fingerprints.

To get perspective on this, look at your fingerprints right now. It may look complex and finite; one might think, "Not much room here for personalization." We are talking about a space no greater than an inch. And when you consider that there has to be billions and billions (or gazillions) of unique patterns to define all the people of the world, it certainly seems like an utterly impossible feat. The level of amazing detail and refinement and crafting and creativity that would have to take place to ensure that no single fingerprint turned out the same is mind-blowing!

But this is the level of detail God went to when he crafted you. He used amazing detail and refinement and crafting to create you exactly as you are. To look exactly as you do. To be exactly who you are. To do exactly what he created you to do.

But let me ask you this. Do you know every detail of your fingerprint? Have you even taken the time to discover it? Can you even see it? (I said while wearing readers . . .)

The likelihood is that you don't know every detail and have not taken much time to discover that unique trait about yourself.

We do this in our lives as well. When it comes to really discovering who we are and our purpose on this planet, we tend to put it in the backseat. Especially when we are paralyzed with a bunch of junk consuming our entire being.

Most people don't come out of the womb knowing these things either. It's not intentional, but worldly ways start shaping us to be who we are and what we do. And somewhere, in that shaping, our godly purpose may be missed.

I'd like to use the example of the iPhone (okay, okay, Galaxy, Pixel . . . whatever your flavor). When you are setting up fingerprint identification, it doesn't just ask you to scan your finger once, does it? No. It scans it several times. Well, have you ever thought about why it does that?

It scans multiple times because it can't take just a portion of your fingerprint to define who you are. Your fingerprint has to be complete for it to fully identify who you are.

Through the course of our lives, that's what we go through as well. We are getting scanned multiple times. Each journey of self-discovery, each tragedy, each victory, each hurdle, each dream, each failure—all are scans revealing more about the fingerprints of our lives. And as we grow with God and each new pattern of our prints is revealed, we grow closer to being complete and fulfilling the purpose he has for our lives.

I like to call God's fingerprint on our hearts our purpose. He tells us that he has given us gifts, and these gifts are given to serve God.

There are different kinds of spiritual gifts, but the same Spirit is the source of them all. There are different kinds of service, but we serve the same Lord. God works in different ways, but it is the same God who does the work in all of us.

1 Corinthians 12:4–7

These fingerprints are what the Bible calls spiritual gifts. In the fourth chapter of the book of Ephesians, Paul breaks this down for us.

Read Ephesians 4.

We have been gifted! Both through the spiritual gift of Jesus Christ but also the gifts he's given us. In Ephesians 4:16, Paul was simply reinforcing what he had already told us. . . . We have been called, and we have special gifts that are to be used.

> *He makes the whole body fit together perfectly.*
> *As each part does its own special work, it helps the*
> *other parts grow, so that the whole body is healthy*
> *and growing and full of love.*

Ephesians 4:16

In this passage, Paul reinforces that our gifts aren't there for our own selfish gain. He gives us spiritual gifts to build up believers. They are to be used to fulfill God's purpose for the benefit of the whole body. In other words, the health of the body is reliant on the use of our spiritual gifts.

Although this can sound pretty scary, it's also really freaking cool. You are that important! God crafted you and created you to help make the whole Christian world go round. Without you and without your gift, there could be wounds going on within the body of Christ that would be untreated. A broken Christian could be without the stint that would heal them. Someone could be waiting for you to perform spiritual CPR on them.

God blew my socks off when he called me to use my gifts and start a ministry to help women. The argument that I ensued with him is still fresh in my brain.

But as I reflect on the last four and a half years and the women I've been able to plant a seed with, it all starts to make sense. God has shown me that the spiritual gift he's given me can and will continue to grow into many beautiful things.

Symbolically, I received a surprise at my door this last week: a bouquet of beautiful flowers. It was not a special occasion, so I knew there was no way they were from my husband. And they weren't.

They were from my friend Kelly. Kelly had been struggling for several years to find a purpose in her career. Despite having a college degree and good experience, she had become paralyzed in believing that she was not qualified to perform a career-level job. She found herself floating around with various part-time jobs for several years, longing for something bigger but terrified to put herself out there.

When a job in her field opened up at the hospital she was working at, she was interested, but the job description was scaring her away. She wasn't looking at how her own gifts could serve in this role but at the qualifications she did not have.

I coached Kelly as she navigated this process, helping her to identify the truth of what she had to offer and dismiss the lies that Satan so desperately wanted her to believe. After all, the big ol' meanie doesn't want anyone to land a job that would leverage their gifts, would he?

Fortunately, Kelly was able to get the courage from God to pursue the job. And land it. She was the woman for the job.

The card in the bouquet she sent me said, "Thank you for believing in me when I didn't."

It wasn't just me who believed in her. It was God. And he used my spiritual gift to help someone else find a way to use theirs. That's what this is all about—living a life called by God to lead others to live a life called by God.

Lead a life worthy of your calling,
for you have been called by God.

Ephesians 4:1

Spiritual Gifts

One thing that cannot be disputed is that if you are a Christian, you have a spiritual gift. Take the check, sign it, and cash it because you can take that truth to the bank.

He has given each one of us a special gift.

Ephesians 4:7

But I realize that some of you might be kind of freaking out at this moment because you don't know what those gifts may be. It's okay. The discovery takes time. And patience.

To look at it from another perspective, think about DNA. Think about what life was like before DNA was discovered. The stories, facts, and truths that were hidden. Everything took greater levels of discovery, research, and time. So many missing pieces.

Researchers spent years going down the wrong paths trying to cure illnesses. They were stuck. They were doing the *wrong* things! They were paralyzed!

But then DNA was discovered, and it changed everything. The entire course of science changed: every research effort, every disease cure, every crime scene. It all changed. Missing pieces found!

The thing is it was there all along.

Nothing changed except the lens that the scientists were looking through.

Our lives are the same—the answers are already within us. We just have to change the lens we are looking through. We have to do the discovery and hard work to seek the truth and find it. By discovering our spiritual gifts manifested by God, we can find our purpose sooner.

> *In his grace, God has given us different gifts for doing certain things well. So if God has given you the ability to prophesy, speak out with as much faith as God has given you. If your gift is serving others, serve them well. If you are a teacher, teach well. If your gift is to encourage others, be encouraging. If it is giving, give generously. If God has given you leadership ability, take the responsibility seriously. And if you have a gift for showing kindness to others, do it gladly.*

Romans 12:6–8

You may recognize a gift listed in the above Scripture. Maybe more than one. If you know how God wants you to use that gift, then do it and give it your all. If you don't know how it is that God wants you to use your gift, it's okay. It's not all going to come to us at once.

Over time, our godly purpose will be revealed. And there are times when we can really feel the missing pieces. But when we find one of those missing pieces, it changes the course of our lives. It changes the way we do things, the way we view things, the way we make decisions.

Every one of us has a godly mission and purpose that contributes to our world. If we find that and follow it with blind faith, it will lead us to our role in making our world a better place and be a beacon of hope to so many.

Pursue the Purpose

Some people confuse their purpose with their passions. These two are *not* the same thing.

When I think of my passions in life, I think of the things that I love more than anything in the world. When I think of my purpose in this world, I think of what I was put on this Earth to do to make the world a better place. There is a place in life for both passions and purpose. And oftentimes, your purpose leverages your passions. But if we stop short at solely engaging in our passions, we might miss the whole reason we are here in the first place.

For a long time, I had no idea what my purpose on Earth was. I knew what I was passionate about. I was passionate about taking care of my family, helping other people, trying to make a difference, speaking, my faith, and being successful. I was doing a good job at pursuing some of those passions, but I wasn't succeeding in them.

- I was financially supporting my family, but I wasn't present in their lives because I was traveling.
- I was helping people when I had the time, but that time was scarce.
- I was a leader in several charitable efforts, but I was not making a significant impact in any of them.
- I was speaking through my job but about stuff that I really didn't care about.
- I was successful doing the "dream job," but I was miserable in it.

I thought I would find fulfillment in pursuing these passions. I thought I would find happiness being in a successful sales career. But I didn't. I came up short. Why?

Because I was not living my purpose.

I was trying to find the success and happiness that the world had influenced. And when I say "world," I'm talking internally and externally.

On the outside, things looked good. On the inside, I was paralyzed with heavy burdens at home. This paralysis made me feel responsible for managing everything in my family's life. And I was fooled into believing that the sexy "dream job" was going to cure it all.

But it didn't. It required me to travel and took me away from my family more and more. I would be gone for a week, sometimes ten days at a time. I missed birthdays, Mother's Days, sports events, children's firsts—days that I will never, ever get back.

Here I was in the middle of what most would call a dream job, traveling, seeing the world, and having experiences people only dream of, and I was miserable. Every part of me felt off. I knew it was not what God wanted for me at all. It was eating away at the things that were most important in my life.

Eventually, God stepped in, and my faith stepped up. God led me down a completely unexpected path, and I started listening. I started following what God was laying on my heart, not my paycheck. I checked my ego at the door and said, "no more!"

Although it seemed utterly crazy to me at the time, I quit the dream job and pursued God, said sayonara to the big pile of money I was making, and never looked back. And as a result, eventually, he took me where I had never even imagined: ministry!

When God revealed that he had a plan for me to minister to women, it didn't go well. I had actually set out in prayer to confirm with God that I should open a sports store in my small town. And instead of confirming that, he dropped that bomb.

It hit me like a bread truck. Never in my life had the thought even crossed my mind. I thought for sure that God had picked the wrong girl.

In fact, I argued with God.

Me: God, I am not what you want. I have too much baggage. I like beer. I curse sometimes. I watch *Bachelor in Paradise*. I am the last person who should minister to people.

God: You are exactly what I want.

Massive panic set in. That argument with God continued for a good half hour, pleading with God that he had it wrong, reminding him of all the reasons why he was wrong, thinking that just maybe, I heard him incorrectly.

But he wasn't wrong. And needless to say, I lost the argument, and God subsequently went to work, and here we are.

Let me tell you this, if God has a purpose of ministry for someone like me, I promise that he has an equally crazy, life-altering, leap-of-faith-requiring, throw-your-plans-out-the-door purpose for you too.

God's purpose transformed my life. He healed me and pursued me. The time I had spent feeding my paralysis of being a survival-focused, financially driven workaholic shifted. It shifted big time into the things most important in my life: being a child of God, a wife, a mom, and an everyday missionary.

He has the same plan for you. This is a biblical truth. You are not meant to be paralyzed. You are meant to have a purpose that uses the spiritual gifts that he's given you.

And what's even more astounding? This is a guaranteed deal he has for you. It does not matter what you've done, how much you've screwed up, or the sinful rap sheet you hold. You cannot lose pursuing God's purpose for your life.

Instead, God will likely use the areas in our lives that hurt as our purpose.

Our lives are not mistakes. Our pasts are not mistakes. Our presents are not mistakes. Our futures are not mistakes. Even the paralysis we are suffering is not a mistake. Instead, God will use the junk in our journeys to fulfill his purpose. He will use you if you tune in and make a choice to listen.

The takeaway for you is this: When we are consumed with paralysis, we are also eating into our capacity to fulfill God's purpose. Something *must* be done about it.

When we reduce or eliminate that paralysis, it allows us to fulfill God's purpose for us. He wants us to use the gifts he has given us. God *needs* us to. His plan requires it. When we take God's purpose for our lives and apply it and live for it, what lines up is God's great plan for us on Earth.

Recovery Questions

It's always been said that change is uncomfortable. And it is true. But when we know that the change is for good, we know we need to be comfortable with the uncomfortable for the time being—and God can help us through that. Take some time to reflect on the following questions.

1. Basic Training

When you think about the struggles in your life, how do they make you feel? Does it make it any better to view them as training for living a better life? Do you want to use your struggles to help others? How can you connect with God to help you identify how he may want to use your struggles?

2. Spiritual Gifts

Do you think that the things that are paralyzing you could be used for good? Do you believe that you have a spiritual gift? What do you think that gift may be? Do you think that your gift could help further the mission of bringing people to Christ?

3. Purpose

Do you see the difference between your passions and your purpose? Do you have an idea of what your godly purpose is? Are you living it right now? If not, what steps can you take to start pursuing it? Envision what pursuing that purpose might look like.

Movement to Move Again

The last few days leading up to finishing this book, I've had trouble breathing. I'm feeling incredibly short of breath. I even used an oxygen sensor and determined my oxygen levels have been low. I feel like I'm suffocating.

I'm pretty healthy right now though. From recent tests I've had run from my hypochondria days, I know that my heart is in great shape. My lungs are good. My health, it's all good.

But I knew. I knew why I was having trouble breathing.

The paralysis of my anxiety was suffocating me.

It's amazing that after writing this entire book, I had not realized some of what I was still carrying with me. God has helped me overcome crippling paralysis in my life. It wouldn't seem like there would be room for much more. But today, in my prayer, I identified a heavy load I was still carrying.

I was still holding on to regrets. Still holding on to guilt. Still holding on to shame.

As I was praying to God on this Good Friday, I found myself at the foot of the cross. And I found myself finally seeing my regrets, my guilt, my shame there with him—something that he took to the grave for me.

This was an emotional prayer for me. I poured the paralysis out to him. I gave it to him completely. I accepted that he has carried it for me. I accepted that my sins are forgiven.

As soon I did that, I found myself taking deep breaths in and out. Breaths of relief and freedom, I'm certain. But in the middle of them, I realized I could breathe again. My breathing issues had subsided. My paralysis was no longer choking me.

When Jesus took his last breath on the cross, it was so your paralysis would no longer suffocate you. He died on the cross so you would no longer have to carry the weight that you've been carrying. Your paralyzing burdens are not yours anymore. He carried those to the cross with him. When he was crucified and died, he took it with him.

Jesus did this for one reason: so we could be set free.

So if the Son sets you free, you are truly free.

John 8:36

It's time to start living in that freedom. The process of *The Paralyzed Movement* is all about finding that freedom. It's about rehabilitating our own lives and getting ourselves to move from the situations in our lives that paralyze us.

As we know, in God's eyes, it's mission-critical that we do. God's purpose relies on us overcoming our paralysis. God paid the greatest price for us to find that freedom.

The Paralyzed Movement doesn't mean you have to find movement on your own. In fact, we know we are in this place because we have been incapable of moving on our own. We need God. He is our answer.

I'll be the first to admit it though, even finding God on our own can be hard.

In both of the stories of Jesus healing the paralyzed, the process of the paralyzed finding healing through him was not done on their own. Quite the contrary. They were healed because of the intervention of the people surrounding them.

In the case of the paralyzed man in Capernaum, he was carried by four men on a mat. I have to imagine that these four men were the paralyzed man's friends. They went above and beyond for him. They dug a hole in a roof for him. Nothing was stopping them from helping their friend get to Jesus. When we need help overcoming the areas in our lives where we are paralyzed, it is ridiculously hard to do it on our own. But when we surround ourselves with followers of Jesus that are willing to carry us through it and to him, it changes the game. It's not just our faith that helps us through life's struggles. It's the faith of others.

In fact, Jesus himself didn't just care about the faith of the paralyzed man. He cared about the faith of all of them.

> *Seeing their faith, Jesus said to the paralyzed man,*
> *"My child, your sins are forgiven."*

Mark 2:5

Seeing *their* faith. Do you see it? Jesus didn't just recognize his faith; he recognized the faith of them all!

The Paralyzed Movement is just that. A movement. To stay on course to finding freedom with God, we must be willing to invite godly people in to help us overcome. And we must be a movement of women helping women to overcome!

Remember Ben, the paralyzed man that Todd and I were certain would never walk again? He had this huge team of people supporting and cheering him on through his journey of paralysis, praying for him, surrounding him.

And what did Ben do? He walked again!

In fact, when Ben walked out of the hospital, he was surrounded by a crowd of fifty people. It was the most significant send-off the hospital had ever seen. Ben was quoted as saying, "I was real emotional seeing all those people there. I just kind of stood there and took it all in," Ben said. "I think I hugged every one of them."

Ben's people played a huge role in his recovery. They believed in him and carried him. They didn't focus on the overwhelming impossibility of him overcoming his paralysis, they focused on the inevitable goal of him walking again.

How many times in our lives do we make judgments about people never being able to overcome the paralyzing burdens in their lives? How many times have you given up hope for someone? How many times have you written someone off?

Have you ever considered that maybe you could be the catalyst to overcoming their challenges? Maybe it's you that could carry them to the cross. Maybe it's you that could help them spiritually walk. We all have a calling to help people walk with Jesus. Our faith in their journey matters too. We must be helping each other. No one should have to struggle through their paralysis alone.

> *Two people are better off than one, for they can help each other succeed. If one person falls, the other can reach out and help. But someone who falls alone is in real trouble.*

Ecclesiastes 4:9–10

Case in point. It wasn't just Jesus that healed the paralyzed in the Bible; he used his disciples. Peter traveled from place to place sharing the good news of Jesus Christ when he came across a paralyzed man named Aeneas.

> *Peter said to him, "Aeneas, Jesus Christ heals you! Get up, and roll up your sleeping mat!" And he was healed instantly.*

Acts 9:34

Peter could have been kicking back in the lap of luxury, enjoying his relationship with the Son of God. Just living the life. But he did not. He spent his days going to help people. Through the power of Jesus Christ, he healed people. He helped someone walk again.

You may not believe this, but God gives you the same power to heal people. By spreading his good news to those who need him, they can find healing. They too can move again.

And what happens in the process of that?

People witness the work of God!

The story of Peter healing Aeneas continued to say:

*The whole population of Lydda and Sharon saw Aeneas
walking around, and they turned to the Lord.*

Acts 9:35

Because of Peter's ministry, people witnessed the healing power of Jesus and turned to the Lord. Do you see the gravity of what that means? These witnesses turned to the Lord and found salvation. Eternal life. A future with God in heaven.

This is why the movement matters! We too can make the same impact that Peter did. It does not matter if we have the ability to physically heal someone. We have the healing power of the word of God to use. We too can help someone find healing. We too can create witnesses of the amazing, miraculous healing power of Jesus Christ, our Savior!

I praise God every day for the opportunity I had to witness the miraculous healing of my husband. And I praise God for the opportunity I've had to witness the miraculous healing he's had in the paralyzed lives of so many others.

But most of all, I praise God for what he's about to do. What he's about to do in your life. What he's about to do in the lives of the people you know. What he's about to do with *The Paralyzed Movement.*

Will you join me in being a part of that movement?

*Jesus turned to the paralyzed man and said, "Stand up,
pick up your mat, and go home!" And immediately, as
everyone watched, the man jumped up, picked up his mat,
and went home praising God. Everyone was gripped with
great wonder and awe, and they praised God, exclaiming,
"We have seen amazing things today!"*

Luke 5:17–26

Join the Movement

Two people are better off than one,
for they can help each other succeed.

Ecclesiastes 4:9

Are you ready to take the next steps in overcoming your paralysis and find others to walk with on your journey?

Visit

www.paralyzedmovement.com

and sign up to receive information on how to get engaged in the movement and resources to help you on your journey.

And, hey, I could use your assistance in helping others find The Paralyzed Movement too!

Please consider leaving a helpful review on Amazon to let other women know what you think of the book.

And while you are at it, please tell all your girlie friends about it!

Just like the woman at the well, Christ needs women who've been paralyzed running to spread the good news to all who will listen. That's what this movement is all about!

Thank you and God bless!

Amanda Zwanziger